# BLACK & DECKER®

# FLOORING 101

# 25 Projects You *Really* Can Do Yourself

## MATTHEW PAYMAR

**Creative Publishing international**

CHANHASSEN, MINNESOTA
www.creativepub.com

**Creative Publishing
international**

Copyright © 2006
Creative Publishing international, Inc.
18705 Lake Drive East
Chanhassen, Minnesota 55317
1-800-328-3895
www.creativepub.com

Printed in China

10 9 8 7 6 5 4 3 2 1

*President/CEO:* Ken Fund
*Publisher:* Bryan Trandem

*Author:* Matthew Paymar
*Editor:* Jennifer Gehlhar
*Art Director:* David Schelitzche
*Cover Design:* Howard Grossman
*Book Design:* Richard Oriolo
*Page Layout:* Joe Fahey
*Assistant Managing Editor:* Tracy Stanley
*Photo Acquisitions Editor:* Julie Caruso
*Production Manager:* Laura Hokkanen

Library of Congress
Cataloging-in-Publication Data

Paymar, Matthew.
Flooring 101 : 25 projects you really can do
yourself / by Matthew Paymar.
    p. cm.
At head of title: Black & Decker.
Summary: "This book features modern flooring
materials and easy-to-follow techniques that will
produce significant improvements with a minimal investment of time and money. Projects
range from eliminating floor squeaks to
installing a laminate flooring system"--Provided
by publisher.
  ISBN-13: 978-1-58923-263-1 (soft cover)
  ISBN-10: 1-58923-263-1 (soft cover)
  1. Flooring. 2. Floors. I. Black & Decker
Corporation (Towson, Md.).
II. Title. III. Title: Black & Decker flooring one
hundred and one.
  TH2521.P39 2006
  690'.16--dc22
                              2006009846

## NOTICE TO READERS

For safety, use caution, care and good judgment when following the procedures described in this book. The Publisher and
Black & Decker cannot assume responsibility for any damage
to property or injury to persons as a result of misuse of the
information provided.

The techniques shown in this book are general techniques for
various applications. In some instances, additional techniques
not shown in this book may be required. Always follow manufacturers' instructions included with products, since deviating
from the directions may void warranties. The projects in this
book vary widely as to skill levels required: some may not be
appropriate for all do-it-yourselfers, and some may require professional help.

Consult your local Building Department for information on
building permits, codes and other laws as they apply to your
project.

# CONTENTS

# Welcome to Flooring 101

FLOORING PLAYS A VITAL ROLE IN THE LOOK AND FEEL OF YOUR HOME. BECAUSE IT IS ONE OF THE LARGEST ELEMENTS IN A ROOM, A FLOOR CREATES INSTANT IMPACT. IT'S IMPORTANT TO ADDRESS BOTH THE FUNCTION AND BEAUTY OF THE FLOORING IN YOUR HOME. AND, OF COURSE, IT'S IMPORTANT TO MAINTAIN THE FLOORS IN YOUR HOME TO GET THE MOST OUT OF THEM.

With this in mind, we've created *Flooring 101*—a unique and enjoyable home repair book. Most repair books, even those that claim to be for beginners, really depend on you already possessing basic knowledge on the subject. What do you do if you have never laid a tile in your life? What if you don't know what a joist is? What if you'd like to silence that mysteriously squeaky floorboard but you don't know where to start?

You reach for *Flooring 101*. This is the one book on simple floor repairs that doesn't assume anything. The step-by-step procedures are accompanied by several tips to make your home flooring repairs a breeze.

1. Help you better understand the basic types of flooring so you can approach repairs with confidence.

2. Teach you basic floor repair by walking you step by step through 25 simple projects.

Whether you're repairing a single broken tile or eyeing sturdy laminates for your kitchen, the tricks of the trade are here. Find out whether you can salvage what you have or if you need to replace it. *Flooring 101* shows you the step-by-step instructions for 25 universal flooring projects in your home. No knowledge is assumed, and no question is left unanswered.

Despite what you might think, or what you might fear, you really don't need a lot of technical understanding to have success at most simple flooring projects. When it gets right down to it, floors have few parts and, if installed correctly, they should give you no problems. As you progress through the book the projects will increase in difficulty. For an added challenge, the last few projects are floor installations.

## HERE'S HOW TO USE THIS BOOK:

The first two pages of each project give you background and technical information that is helpful to fully understand the project. Everything needed to complete the project is shared up front: skills needed, time needed, terms you need to know, and the tools and supplies needed.

Turn the page to find step-by-step instructions to accomplish the task at hand. Virtually every step is photographed so you can see exactly how to do the work. Along the way you'll also find helpful sidebars that show you what to do if something unexpected happens, tips for using tools correctly, safety recommendations, and more. Before you know it, your DIY floor repair will be a success.

It's that easy. Really.

Let's get to work.

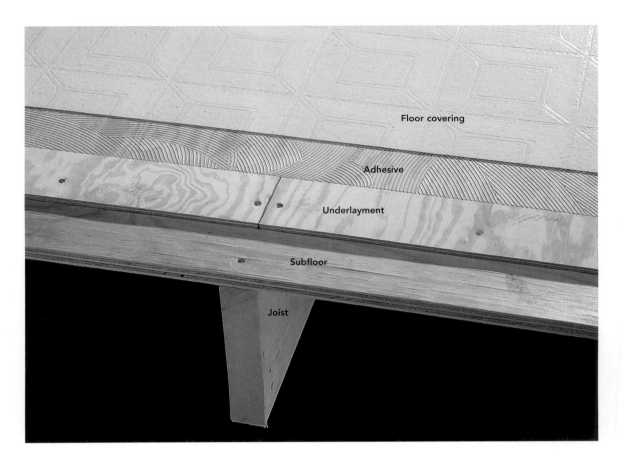

Floor covering

Adhesive

Underlayment

Subfloor

Joist

## ANATOMY OF A FLOOR

When most of us think of a floor we envision the top layer: in effect, the decorative covering—hardwood, ceramic tile, laminate, or carpet. The "real" floor is hidden underneath.

Your floor is made of a sturdy plywood or composite panel subfloor that spans supportive floor joists. The subfloor may be large sheets or planks (and the planks may be arranged in a staggered or diagonal fashion). The joists sit on sills along the foundation and are often supported at a midpoint by a steel girder or wood beam.

An elevated framed floor, like the one shown above, is supported by beams that run perpendicular to the joists. In most cases, the joists are tied together with bridging for extra stability (see photo, lower right).

Depending on the type of flooring used, the subfloor may be covered with an additional layer of underlayment, such as a cement board. The top layer of flooring is installed on the underlayment or subfloor and may rest on some type of cushioning layer, such as roofing felt. Of course, there are always custom options, such as soundproofing or heating, that may be layered into your floor plan. It's important to know what is under your floor covering and how your floor is supported before starting any repairs on that floor.

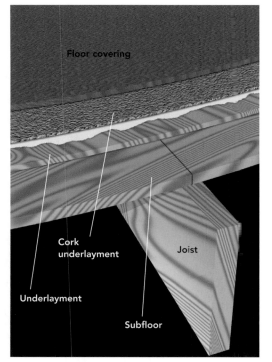

Soundproofed floors have an extra layer to damper noise. When patching a damaged area of your floor, replace the floor covering on top of the sound barrier material. The sound barrier is not altered.

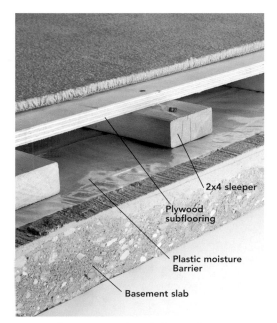

Basement floors are uniquely layered to compensate for the hard concrete base. When patching your damaged floor, only remove the floor covering on top of the plywood subfloor.

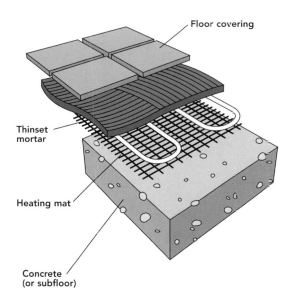

Radiant floor heating systems use hot water coils or electricity. Even concrete floors without floor covering may be heated.

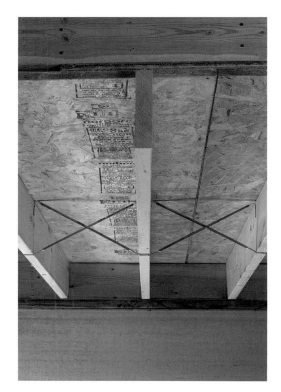

The bridging tied to joists for extra stability could be wood or metal.

Today's homeowner is faced with an extensive range of flooring choices. Selecting the right floor can almost be harder than installing it.

If installing new floors, it is fun to choose the colors, patterns, and other design qualities of the floor you desire. But there are some other qualities to consider, including: cost, comfort, ease of maintenance, and durability.

The varying characteristics of the floors discussed here will help you decide which floor is best for your space. For example, hard flooring—such as ceramic tiles or concrete—is tough, attractive, and great for high-traffic areas. Soft floors, like carpet, are still popular in both bedrooms and living areas because they offer comfort, warmth, and a feeling of luxury.

If your floors are already installed—often homes have four or more types of flooring—the following discussion will help you recognize their strong points. Knowing what your floor can handle helps with maintenance, decorating, and cleaning.

Parquet tile floors offer the beauty and feel of wood in the block shape of tiles. Decorative patterns make these floors appear to be high end when they are actually quite affordable. All parquet tiles feature tongue-and-groove edges that snap together. You can find parquet tiles with self-adhesive backs, but dry-back tiles to which you apply standard flooring adhesive stay put longer.

Concrete floors are typically found in basements and garages for obvious reasons. They are tough and can withstand high traffic, heavy equipment, messy spills (including sitting water), scratches, and scuffs. But concrete is increasingly popular for interior spaces, especially when finished with paint or decorative acid stains.

Laminate floors are available in planks or squares. They snap together with tongue-and-groove joints and then "float" on top of the floor, meaning they are not fastened directly to the subfloor or underlayment. A laminate floor consists of a very durable surface-wear layer; a photographic print layer, which allows it to replicate the appearance of other surfaces; and a solid core.

Ceramic tile floors look spectacular, and they are durable. At the same time, they tend to be cold, they conduct sound, and they are expensive. Upon installation, they are evenly spaced (see plastic spacers in photo) and then the joints are filled with grout. These joints are then sealed.

Manufactured wood flooring materials include: fiberboard surfaced with a synthetic laminate layer (right), plywood topped with a thin hardwood veneer (center), and parquet tile made of wood strips (left). Wood floors come in planks or strips. The planks fit together with tongue-and-groove joints or square edges and, depending on manufacturer recommendations, they float on top of the subfloor or are secured in place with nails, staples, and/or glue.

Resilient floors include vinyl, linoleum, cork, and rubber. They are comfortable underfoot and easy to clean. They are impervious to water—except at the seams or where torn. Depending upon the material, resilient flooring comes in either large sheets, which need to be cut to size, or easy-to-install tiles. Resilient floors are often cost effective and are available in a staggering number of patterns and colors. They are usually thin, which means the subfloor must be level.

Carpet is the most popular choice for living rooms and bedrooms because it produces a warm, comfortable environment. It is available in conventional, cushion-back, or tile forms. Wall-to-wall carpet is laid with fittings, such as tackless strips and padding. Cushion-backed carpet is glued directly to the subfloor.

# Before You Begin: Evaluating Floors

Floor coverings wear out faster than other interior surfaces because they get more wear and tear. Surface damage can affect more than just appearance. Scratches in resilient flooring and cracks in grouted tile joints allow moisture to wear away at adhesive, eventually pushing up the floor covering or tile. Hardwood floors lose their finish and become discolored. And loose floorboards squeak. If that problem appears to be minor now, the question is: Clean, repair, or replace?

Before answering that question, you must thoroughly inspect your entire floor. Depending on the type of floor, look for stains, tears, rips, cracks, buckles, bubbles, or damp spots. Specific concerns for each type of flooring material are listed in this section. Once the problem is classified, you may move on to the repair project specific to the problem.

Concrete floors are hard and durable, but still require care. If unsealed, concrete is vulnerable to all kinds of stains. Oil and grease are particularly troublesome. Cracks are also common. *Flooring 101* shows you how to tackle both of these issues.

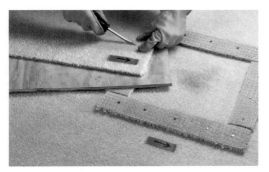

Look for tears, stains, or excessive wear in carpet. Cleaning the spots should always be the first step, and there are carpet-cleaning products for almost every possible stain (see page 24). If this doesn't do the trick, these damaged areas may be fixed with a patch (as shown in photo).

Dirt is the primary enemy of laminate floors. If your floor is dull or has visible scratches, it is probably the result of years of accumulated dirt from foot traffic. Unfortunately, this is unavoidable. Often touch-up sticks are available from the manufacturer to repair scratches. A severely damaged tile or plank may be completely removed (as is being done in photo) and replaced.

Moisture can cause wood floors to buckle. To detect buckled floors early on, check your floor with a level. Buckled planks should be removed so you can inspect the subfloor. Allowing the subfloor to dry out allows you to then replace new, tight-fitting planks.

Though quite durable, parquet tiles are still vulnerable to stains, especially from heavy spills or water that sits on the floor for some time. It is important to clean up spills immediately (see page 14). If necessary, individual tiles may be removed and replaced.

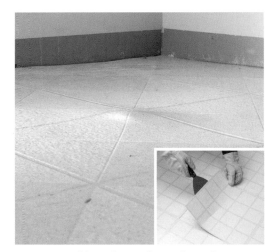

Even durable ceramic tiles develop signs of wear. To evaluate ceramic tiles, check for loose, cracked, or dirty grout joints. It is definitely worth removing an individual tile to regrout a damaged joint.

A common problem for resilient sheet floors is air bubbles. To remove bubbles, see page 44. For resilient tiles (inset), the most common repair is loose seams. Tiles with small curls may be reattached (see page 47), but tiles with dirt under them must be completely removed and replaced (see page 48).

# Cleaning Hard Floors

**1**

Even the most durable wood floors are susceptible to stains from liquid spills. To ensure lasting beauty, it's important to clean up spills on the spot and to follow the right procedures, depending on your floor type and spill.

A CLEAN FLOOR IS AN INDICATION OF A WELL-MAINTAINED FLOOR. AS WE might strive for a floor "clean enough to eat on," that's quite a lofty dream. After all, floors are landing spots for gym bags, pet bottoms, and baby urps. Our floors are splash pans for all sorts of spills. It is absolutely necessary to regularly clean and inspect your floors to prevent spills or damage from becoming significant repairs.

# HARD FLOOR CLEANING 101

Routine cleaning tools for wood, ceramic tiles, and concrete floors (from left to right): wet mop, dry mop, broom, handheld broom with dustpan, stiff bristle push broom, fine bristle push broom. A dry mop is good for picking up dust and fine particles and may be used daily. For cleaning joints and room corners, use a small handheld broom. On smooth surfaces, use a household broom, fine bristle push broom, or canister vacuum with bare floor attachments. On rough surfaces (including outdoor or garage concrete) use a stiff bristle push broom or shop vac. Every month or so it is good to damp mop concrete or ceramic tiles.

## TERMS YOU NEED TO KNOW

SURFACE FINISH—Wood floor finish that provides a durable coating (for example, polyurethane (oil- or water-based) varnish, shellac, and lacquer).

PENETRANT FINISH—Penetrant floor finishes seep into the wood pores and become an integral part of the wood (for example, stains or sealers).

STAINS—Penetrants that alter the natural color of the wood. They can be used with a surface finish or protected with a sealer and wax.

SEALERS—Clear or tinted penetrants. Must be covered with wax or surface finish.

WAX—Wood floors without a surface finish need a coat of liquid, non-water based wax. Periodically, this wax needs to be reapplied.

GROUT—A very fine cement mortar used to fill the joints between ceramic tiles.

GROUT SEALER—A silicone sealer used to seal grout lines.

Kitty litter (concrete only)

Bleach

Hydrogen peroxide

Mineral spirits

Lye

Soap with TSP

Steel wool

Sandpaper

Mop with bucket

Household vinegar

Ammonia

Wax

Flexible spatula

Wet/dry vacuum

Power washer

Canister vacuum

## SKILLS YOU NEED

- Vacuuming
- Mopping
- Working with strong cleaners

## DIFFICULTY LEVEL

SKILLS LEVEL

EASY          MODERATE

These projects can be completed in as little as 10 minutes.

# CLEANING WOOD FLOORS

Immediately clean spills with a dry cloth. Allow the cloth to soak up liquid spills. Avoid rubbing the spill into the floor. Once the spill is soaked up, use a damp cloth to blot the remaining residue on the floor. Rinse your cloth often and thoroughly wring it out before using it again. Use a dry, clean cloth to dry the area when you are done. If it is still sticky, allow the area to dry and then use a damp mop (see photo caption to the right). Take care to only clean as needed. Over-cleaning discolors the finish.

As a last resort, stubborn sticky floors need to be wet mopped. Only wet mop the floor if the finish is in good condition. A sponge mop moistened with a mixture of water and a mild wood floor cleaner or a neutral pH soap or detergent (1 gal.: ½ cup cleaner) is all that is required. The mop should just barely be damp at any given time. Excess water can seriously damage wood floors. After cleaning, use a towel to thoroughly dry the floor.

If a liquid spill fades your hardwood floor, lightly sand the damaged area and apply new finish. Do not use a wax finish over a surface finish. See page 31 to determine what type of finish is on your floor.

See page 31 to determine what type of finish is on your floor.

## WHAT IF . . . ?

If you have manufactured flooring, follow the cleaning recommendations provided by the manufacturer. Many manufacturers caution against using water or any cleaner that's mixed with water.

Use nonmarking floor protectors on your furniture's "feet." Sets often include nails or screws to attach the feet. There are also special protectors for wheels. Be sure to buy the correct size and style for your furniture.

After vacuuming the entire room with a bare-floor canister vacuum, use special hardwood floor attachments for corners and the floor perimeter, where dust clumps often settle.

## HERE'S HOW

Make sure you know what sort of finish (wax or urethane) is on your wood floor (see page 31), and use products specifically for your floor surface. Look for products labeled "for wood floor cleaning," for example. Avoid ammonia products or soaps with oil; use pH-balanced cleaners for routine cleaning.

## MAINTENANCE TIPS—WOOD FLOOR

| DAMAGE | QUICK FIX |
| --- | --- |
| MINOR SCRATCHES | WAXED FLOORS—Apply a coat of wax (matching that already on the floor) and buff. |
| | POLYURETHANE FLOORS—Touch-up kits are available at most home centers and hardware stores. |
| FOOD STAINS | Blot the stain with a damp cloth; if necessary, gently scrape food chunks off the floor with a plastic spatula. |
| DARK SPOTS (INK, PET STAINS) | On a polyurethane-finished or wax-finished floor, remove the floor finish with #2 steel wool and then use a finish-specific wood cleaner or mineral spirits. Wash the area with some household vinegar. If that doesn't work, lightly sand the area with fine sandpaper until the stain is gone; clean up dust with a tack cloth; stain, if required; and refinish with matching polyurethane or wax finish. The darker the stain, the deeper it is. To replace a floorboard, see page 80. |
| OIL AND GREASE | WAXED FLOORS—Soak up spilled oil or grease immediately. First blot the area with a dry cloth and then use a slightly damp cloth. If residue remains, wash the area with lye soap. |
| | POLYURETHANE FLOORS—Apply mineral spirits or soap with trisodium phosphate (TSP) to a soft cloth and gently rub until the stain is gone. |
| MOLD OR MILDEW | Clean with an approved cleaner for your specific floor finish. On waxed floors, you may need to rub with #1 steel wool, then rewax and buff. |
| SURFACE DAMAGE | Damage such as water or burn marks and scratches and gouges should be repaired immediately. Strip wax or oil finish by rubbing the floor with fine-grade steel wool or sandpaper. Once smooth, rewax or refinish. |

Protect garage floors during car maintenance. When changing oil, use scraps of cardboard and newspapers to protect the floor from spills. For spilled windshield washer fluid, rinse floor with water and a wet mop. Occasionally air out garages and allow wet floors to dry.

Sweep your floor once a week or more, as needed. For daily maintenance of home interior concrete surfaces, make a quick pass over the floor with a dry mop.

Use a power sprayer and a stiff bristle broom to lift sticky messes in garages. Allow the concrete to dry and then use the stiff bristle broom to sweep remaining dirt out of the garage. For indoor spaces, use a warm damp mop. Rinse the mop out frequently. Warm water lifts grime from the concrete surface. You may also use a specialty steam machine (make sure it is not a commercial deep cleaner; they often incorporate a shampoo feature).

After using a power sprayer to clean concrete floors, use a wet/dry vac to clean up standing water and leftover debris. Vacuuming dry floors is a good addition to weekly sweeping. Use a canister machine for bare floors in interior living spaces and a large shop vac for garages. Use hoses for large clumps of debris.

**PRO TIP**

To make sure your wet mop is ready to be used the next time you need it, rinse it out after each use. Allow it to completely dry before storing it away. Hang it in a cool, dry storage room. Replace mop heads as needed. And never leave a wet mop in the bucket.

Once your concrete floor is clean, look for problem areas. Clean out cracks with a stiff wire brush or a wire wheel on a portable drill. Too patch and seal, refer to page 64.

## MAINTENANCE TIPS—CONCRETE FLOOR

| DAMAGE | QUICK FIX |
| --- | --- |
| GREASE AND OIL | Absorb with unscented cat litter. Sweep the oil-soaked litter onto newspaper. Throw the newspaper in a plastic bag and seal it. Dispose this bag as hazardous waste. Now you can scrub the area with hot liquid dish soap and water, or laundry soap and water. Blot dry with towels and dispose rags as hazardous waste. Alternatively, try commercial concrete degreaser. |
| DARK STAINS | Use diluted household bleach. Or dilute one cup of trisodium phosphate (TSP) in one gallon of hot water. Use a cloth soaked in the bleach to wipe the area clean. |
| MOLD OR MILDEW | Mix 1 part bleach with 3 parts warm water and let the mixture sit on the nasty patch of floor until the mold lifts. Wipe the area clean with a dry towel. |
| RUST | Use 1 part sodium citrate to 6 parts glycerin. Use a cloth to wash the area. |
| COPPER, BRONZE, OR INK | Use 1 part ammonia to 9 parts water. Use a cloth to wash the area. |
| IRON | Use 1 part oxalic acid to 9 parts water. Use a cloth to wash the area. |
| LATEX PAINT | Use a scraper to loosen large chunks. Dip a stiff brush into soapy water and scrub. |
| OIL-BASED PAINT | Use a commercial paint remover or mineral spirits. Use a cloth to rub the area clean. |

Caution! When working with acids or other strong cleaners, always wear long sleeves and pants, rubber gloves, and safety goggles. Make sure the work area is well ventilated.

To gently remove particles that could scratch your tile, dry mop daily.

Vacuum grout joints with a bare-floor attachment once a week. Use a soft-bristle broom or handheld broom and dustpan to pick up debris that the vacuum missed. To eliminate mildew or mold, see the chart (page 19). If dirt or sand is a regular problem, try to find out how it is tracked in. Place rugs or mats at those entryways. Be sure to regularly shake out the rugs.

Use pH-balanced cleaners or soapless detergents for bi-weekly mopping. Having a bucket with a wringer helps to ensure you do not oversaturate the mop. Alternatively, use a sponge mop with an attachment to wring out sponge. Always dry mop or vacuum first. If you prefer not to use commercial cleaning products, use a steam cleaner (be sure not to buy a deep cleaner, which often incorporates shampoo).

## HERE'S HOW

Add glass cleaner to the water in your cleaning bucket to prevent streaks from showing up once the floor is dry. If the floor has a dull finish, it may be time to reseal the floor. If water absorbs into the grout lines, the grout joints need to be resealed. It is still necessary to clean the floor before sealing.

If water doesn't bead on tiles or on grout joints during regular cleaning, it's time to apply another coat of sealer. For instructions on grouting and sealing ceramic tile joints, see page 70.

For heavy stains on natural stone tile, try a manufacturer poultice specifically for porous stone materials. Cover the stain with the poultice, then tape plastic over it. Let the poultice set, according to the manufacturer's instructions, then remove it.

## MAINTENANCE TIPS—CERAMIC TILE FLOOR

| DAMAGE | QUICK FIX |
|---|---|
| DISCOLORATION | For grout joints, use oxygen bleach powder with water. Allow the solution to sit for at least 30 minutes. Gently scrub the area with a cloth or sponge. Rinse the floor with a damp mop. Allow the floor to dry. |
| GREASE | Sponge or brush with water and household cleaner. Avoid ammonia products. |
| BLOOD, COFFEE, JUICE, WINE, MUSTARD | Make a paste of water and baking soda and apply it to the stain. If that doesn't do it, apply oxygen bleach and water. Allow the mixture to sit for at least 30 minutes. Rinse with a damp mop. Rinse several times to remove the cleaning product, but do not get the floor too wet. Use a towel to dry the floor. |
| LATEX PAINT | Gently scrape off what you can without scratching the tile. Scrub remaining paint with soap and water. Rinse thoroughly. |
| OIL-BASED PAINT | Use paint remover. If you use harsh chemicals on your tile, be sure to wash and rinse the area after cleaning. You may need to apply new sealer to the area as well. |
| RUST OR MINERAL DEPOSITS | Use products specifically designed for removing these stains from the ceramic tiles. |
| MILDEW OR MOLD | Scrub the stain on white grout with an old toothbrush dipped in full-strength bleach (don't use with colored grout; use a commercial product instead). |

Always check for products specifically designed for your type of flooring before using generic household cleaners. Inappropriate cleaners can strip sealer from the floor. Also, always let your floor completely dry after following the cleaning steps above and then apply a sealer.

Caution! When working with acids or other strong cleaners, always wear long sleeves and pants, rubber gloves, and safety goggles. Make sure the work area is well ventilated.

# Cleaning Resilient & Laminate Floors

## 2

Keeping a resilient or laminate floor clean is the key to maintaining its beauty and function. Many come with water- and stain-resistant finishes, which makes your job that much easier.

RESILIENT AND LAMINATE FLOORS OFFER EASY MAINTENANCE, VERSATILITY, warmth, colorful options, and beauty. And every year advanced new offerings in this realm become more sophisticated, making these floors easier to maintain. Often the surface layer is already treated with a finish, protecting the floor and making maintenance that much easier from the moment it is installed.

# RESILIENT & LAMINATE 101

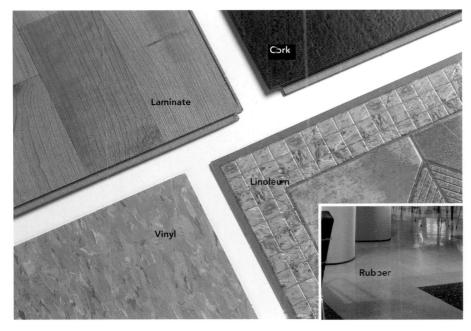

Laminate

Cork

Linoleum

Vinyl

Rubber

Identify your floor type and existing surface finish (you may need to contact the manufacturer to determine the surface finish); then follow the manufacturer's instructions for that floor. Most manufacturers have cleaning kits with instructions. And laminate floor warranties, which can be as long as 20 years, require certain maintenance procedures.

## TERMS YOU NEED TO KNOW

LAMINATE—This flooring is constructed of several layers—including a photographic layer, which mimics the appearance of other floor coverings such as wood, tile, and stone. It is easy to maintain and resists scratches.

RESILIENT—Flooring that comes in a variety of materials, but vinyl is by far the most common and usually the most economical choice today.

VINYL—This flooring is a synthetic product. It comes in sheets or composite tiles and is often coated with strong, long-lasting coverings to resist stains and tears.

LINOLEUM—Linseed oil and cork dust laid on a backing of canvas. Linoleum also comes in sheets or tiles.

CORK—A renewable resource product from the bark of the cork oak, it is usually made with tongue-and-groove joints to secure the planks or tiles together. It has a moisture-resistant inner core. Often, it is finished with a vinyl layer to help protect the cork and make cleaning easier.

SEALERS—Penetrants that alter the natural color of the wood. They can be used with a surface finish or protected with a sealer and wax.

RUBBER—A highly resilient, extremely low-maintenance flooring material available in tiles or sheets. It is sound absorbent, recyclable, and durable.

## SKILLS YOU NEED

• Vacuuming
• Mopping
• Using a flexible spatula
• Working with strong cleaners

## DIFFICULTY LEVEL

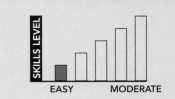

SKILLS LEVEL

EASY          MODERATE

These projects can be completed in as little as 10 minutes.

# CLEANING RESILIENT FLOORS

Remove tough stains with mineral spirits or household bleach. Wet a rag with the solution, and place it over the stain. Lay a plastic bag over the rag to slow evaporation. Wait 1 to 2 hours, then wipe up the stain. Always test solvents in an inconspicuous area before using them elsewhere on the floor. Bleach may strip the protective finish off the floor, leaving it dull. If this happens, refinish.

Occasionally wet mop. Regular dry mopping and vacuuming is necessary, but it doesn't remove sticky spots. Sometimes all that is necessary is a little warm water. Also be sure to inspect seams in tile and the perimeter of full-spread sheet flooring. Use a slightly damp cloth to pick up dirt or dust stuck in seams or corners—especially around thresholds, where material tends to settle after sweeping.

## MAINTENANCE TIPS—RESILIENT FLOOR

| DAMAGE | QUICK FIX |
| --- | --- |
| WAX | Carefully scrape the wax off the floor with a plastic scraper. If the wax is stubborn, follow the directions for wax in the chart for laminate floors. |
| CRAYON | Dab a cloth in mineral spirits or the manufacturer's cleaner and scrub the area clean. Use a damp cloth to rinse the area after the crayon lifts. |
| FRUIT JUICE, WINE, MUSTARD | Wipe the area with a cloth dabbed in full-strength bleach or a manufacturer's cleaner. If you use bleach, be sure to rinse until the surface is shining again. |
| HEEL MARKS | Rub with a cloth dabbed in a nonabrasive cleaner. |
| INK | Rub with a cloth dabbed in citrus-based cleaner or rubbing alcohol. |
| NAIL POLISH | Rub with a cloth dabbed in acetone-based nail polish remover. Use a damp cloth to rinse the area. |
| PAINT | While still wet, soak up paint with a dry cloth. Next, wipe the area with a cloth dabbed in mineral spirits. If dry, scrape the paint off with a plastic scraper and then wipe away the remaining paint with a cloth dabbed in rubbing alcohol. |
| PERMANENT MARKER | Rub the stain with a cloth dabbed in mineral spirits, nail polish remover, or rubbing alcohol. Use a damp cloth to rinse the area. |
| RUST | Mix 1 part oxalic acid to 10 parts water; carefully follow the acid manufacturer's directions, as this is an extremely caustic solution. |
| SHOE POLISH | Dab a cloth in a citrus-based cleaner or mineral spirits and rub the area. |

Caution! Wear long sleeves, rubber gloves, and goggles.

# CLEANING LAMINATE FLOORS

If your floor is dull even after you clean it, you should polish. Put manufacturer polish into a clean bucket, dip a cloth into it, and wring about half the polish out of the cloth. Working in a 3- to 4-ft. square, wipe the cloth over the floor in straight lines. Apply 2 to 3 coats; let the polish dry for at least 30 minutes between coats and about an hour (minimum) when you're done.

On vinyl and laminate, you can remove tough spots like shoe polish or tar with nail polish remover containing acetone. When the spot is gone, wipe the area with a clean, damp cloth.

## MAINTENANCE TIPS—LAMINATE FLOOR

| DAMAGE | QUICK FIX |
|---|---|
| WAX | Place a paper towel on the wax and lay an old towel over this. Set a warm clothing iron on the towel for a few seconds, just until the wax warms. Scrape the wax up with the plastic scraper or putty knife. |
| CRAYON, HEEL MARKS | Rub with a dry cloth or a bit of acetone. Rinse the area with a damp cloth. |
| FRUIT JUICE, WINE | Rub with a dry cloth or a bit of commercial cleaner on a cloth. Rinse the area with a damp cloth. |
| LIPSTICK | Rub with a cloth just barely dabbed in acetone or paint thinner. |
| NAIL POLISH | Dab a cloth in acetone-based nail polish remover and scrub the area; then rinse with a damp cloth. |
| PAINT | While still wet, clean up latex paint with a damp cloth. If dry, scrape the paint off the floor with a plastic scraper. |
| INK, TAR, SHOE POLISH | Scrub with a cloth dabbed in acetone or paint thinner. Rinse the area with a damp cloth. |

Caution! Wear long sleeves, rubber gloves, and goggles.

# Cleaning Carpet

## 3

A good vacuum cleaner or central vacuum system is your first line of defense in maintaining the beauty of your carpet. You should vacuum at least twice a month. If possible, make sure your carpet has stain resistance built in and is a color or pattern suitable for its use in your home.

RARE, IF EVEN EXISTENT, WOULD BE THE HOUSEHOLD WITH SPOTLESS CARPET. This luxurious, soft, quiet, beautiful floor covering is susceptible to all manner of woes and calamities in any normal home with foot traffic. You could allow only stocking feet. No eating or drinking. No pets. Vacuum at least once a day. . . . But dust still settles. Furniture legs make dents. And sunlight streams in, fading or discoloring your otherwise beautiful carpet. As you can understand, regular cleaning is a must.

# CARPET CLEANING 101

| Deep cleaner | Bagless | Stick | Upright |
| --- | --- | --- | --- |
| | | Handheld | Canister |

Using the correct vacuum for the job at hand is important. Above are some of the vacuums recommended for routine maintenance.

## TERMS YOU NEED TO KNOW

**HANDHELD**—Small vacuums that are often rechargeable or battery operated.

**CANISTER**—Lightweight vacuums that are often geared toward bare floors.

**STICK**—Slim vacuum with subtle suction. These vacuums are smaller and do not have the suction power of standard uprights. They are good for small spaces.

**UPRIGHT**—Good for wall-to-wall carpet with few obstacles.

**LIGHTWEIGHT**—These vacuums are specifically designed to be portable. They often have straight suction.

**BAGLESS**—Dirt and dust is contained in a removable container, which is often plastic. It eliminates the need for commercial bags.

**STEAMER**—This is a machine that uses the steam from hot water to loosen and then lift residue. Pure steam cleaners are not used on carpet as often as hard or resilient surfaces. For carpet, you can call in a professional to steam or use a commercial deep cleaner.

**DEEP CLEANER**—Shampoo or water-extraction (also called "steam cleaning") machine that loosens residue with hot water and steam and then lifts it off the carpet, storing the dirty water in a separate tank that must occasionally be emptied. Most commercial products now combine both shampoo and steam (or "heat" features) into one machine.

**CENTRAL SYSTEM**—Tubing inside walls direct dirt and debris to a receptable (usually in the basement or garage). Inlets around the home allow you to plug in a lightweight hose.

## TOOLS & SUPPLIES YOU NEED

Water
Club soda
H₂O
Carpet cleaner
Mild detergent
Vinegar
Iron
Hair dryer
Ice cubes
Sponge
Clean cloth
Dull kitchen knife
Razorblades
Steel wool

## SKILLS YOU NEED

- Vacuuming
- Using a deep cleaner
- Using a dull knife

## DIFFICULTY LEVEL

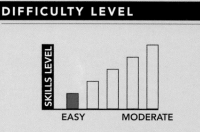

SKILLS LEVEL

EASY          MODERATE

This project can be completed in as little as 10 minutes or as much as 2 hours.

Use a large spoon to pick up spills. Spoons capture liquids well without damaging fibers. Scoop toward the center of the stain to avoid spreading. Do not rub stains—blot them (see inset). Apply cleaning solution to a cloth or paper towel, then blot the stain, working from the outside toward the center to avoid spreading the stain.

Every machine has slightly different features, but most commercial deep cleaning products available today operate by the same principles. To deep clean your carpet push the machine forward over a 3-ft. square area, releasing the detergent and rotating the brush. At this time hot water is often used, causing steam. When you pull back, cold water is used as a rinse. Some machines allow you to manually adjust the water temperature. Always be sure to rinse thoroughly. Slowly go over the same area a couple of times to work the cleaner into the carpet. Repeat this process until the entire carpet is cleaned. Allow the carpet to dry. Vacuum.

## PRO TIP

It usually takes a day for carpet to dry. Wait at least this long before replacing furniture.

Raise crushed fibers by first dampening the area with water (or allow a small ice cube to melt on each dent overnight). Work up the crushed fibers with your hand (or a spoon, if they are stubborn). A hair dryer on medium temperature not only helps dry the spots while you raise the fibers, but the heat helps raise the fibers. Sometimes simply holding a steam iron above the dent will pop up the crushed carpet.

There may be more homegrown remedies for carpet spot removal than there are types of carpet. Perhaps the most ubiquitous of these remedies is club soda, alleged to cure stains from red wine to coffee and ketchup. This inexpensive carbonated drink mixer is known to lift stains to the surface so you can blot them up, while the salts help prevent staining. Whether you use home remedies or commercial products, always do a test in an inconspicuous area to make sure you don't bleach or stain your carpet.

Manufacturers have recommendations for cleaning products. Always check with your carpet manufacturer first, and adhere to their recommendations.

| DAMAGE | QUICK FIX |
|---|---|
| ALCOHOLIC BEVERAGES, CANDY, CHOCOLATE, EGGS, FRUIT JUICE, GRAVY, KETCHUP, MUSTARD, SYRUP, SOFT DRINKS, URINE | Combine water, club soda, and vinegar—or use a carpet spot cleaner or shampoo. Depending on the type of carpet you have, follow the manufacturer's directions. Repeatedly blot the area to lift the stain. Allow the carpet to completely dry and then vacuum. |
| BUTTER, MARGARINE, CRAYONS, FURNITURE POLISH, GREASE, MOTOR OIL, PERFUME, SALAD DRESSING, VEGETABLE OIL, SHOE POLISH, TAR | Apply a dry cleaner; if traces remain, apply a carpet shampoo product. Blot the stain with the cleaning product and then blot again with water to remove cleaning product residue. Allow the carpet to dry and then vacuum. |
| BLOOD, EXCREMENT, VOMIT | Sponge with cool water; add carpet shampoo and ammonia or white vinegar. Blot the area until the stain lifts. To remove cleaning residue, blot the area with water. Allow the carpet to dry and then vacuum. |
| CHEWING GUM | Chill the gum with ice cubes. With a dull knife, scrape off as much as possible. Blot area with a cloth and dry cleaner. Use a damp cloth to soak up the cleaning residue. Rinse the cloth frequently. Let dry. Vacuum. |
| CANDLE WAX | Chill with ice cubes and scrape off as much as possible with a dull knife. Put paper towels and brown paper over stain; iron on medium heat to soak up wax. Apply dry cleaner, if necessary. |
| NAIL POLISH | Wipe fresh spills with mild detergent and water. Don't use nail polish remover, it will dissolve polyester fibers. If the spill has set, try steam cleaning. |
| BURN MARKS | If only tips of the fiber are scorched, carefully scrape away the scorched portion using a fine, steel wool pad or razorblade. |

# Repairing Splinters

## 4

Ouch! If a floorboard begins to splinter, it's a good idea to repair it before the splinter completely dislodges and disappears—or worse, completely dislodges into someone's bare foot.

IT IS COMMON FOR SPLINTERS TO APPEAR IN FLOORS THAT ARE DRIED OUT and brittle. When hardwood floors are damaged by high heels or pushed chair legs, a portion of the grain may dislodge; because the grain of wood runs only in one direction, it splinters rather than simply creating a hole. Floorboards that have splinters or gouges don't necessarily have to be replaced; a splinter can be reattached with some glue and a hole can be filled with some wood putty.

# WOOD SPLINTERS 101

Fiberboard

Plywood

Parquet

All types of wood—both manufactured and hardwood—are susceptible to splinters and small holes. Whether you have parquet tiles or antique hardwood planks, you can fix these problems.

## TERMS YOU NEED TO KNOW

RECONDITIONING FLOORS—Lightly sanding only the finish of the floor (to dull the surface) and then reapplying a new coat of finish.

FEATHER SAND—Sanding with lighter and lighter strokes as you move away from a more heavily sanded area. This creates a smooth transition between sanded and non-sanded areas.

## TOOLS & SUPPLIES YOU NEED

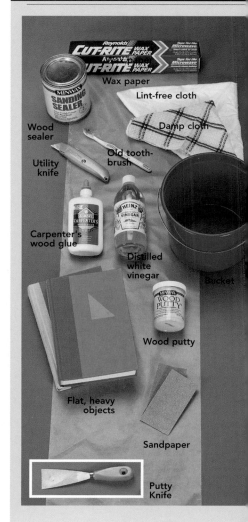

Wax paper

Lint-free cloth

Wood sealer

Damp cloth

Old toothbrush

Utility knife

Carpenter's wood glue

Distilled white vinegar

Bucket

Wood putty

Flat, heavy objects

Sandpaper

Putty Knife

## SKILLS YOU NEED

- Gluing
- Using a putty knife
- Sanding
- Applying a top coat (polyurethane and wax)

## DIFFICULTY LEVEL

SKILLS LEVEL

EASY          MODERATE

This project can be completed in less than an hour (not including drying time).

# HOW TO GLUE DOWN A SPLINTER

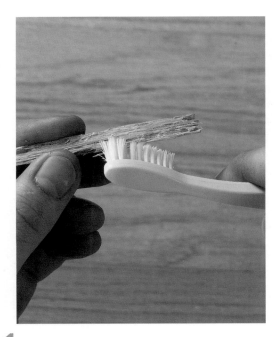

**1** If you still have the splintered piece of wood, but it has been entirely dislodged from the floor, it's a good bet that the hollowed space left by the splinter has collected a lot of dirt and grime. Combine a 1:3 mixture of distilled white vinegar and water in a bucket. Dip an old toothbrush into the solution and use it to clean out the hole left in the floor. While you're at it, wipe down the splinter with the solution, too. Allow the floor and splinter to thoroughly dry.

**2** If the splinter is large, apply wood glue to the hole and splinter. Use a Q-tip or toothpick to apply small amounts of wood glue under smaller splinters. Soak the Q-tip in glue; you don't want Q-tip fuzz sticking out of your floor once the glue dries.

**3** Press the splinter back into place. To clean up the excess glue, use a slightly damp, lint-free cloth. Do not oversoak the cloth with water.

**4** Allow the adhesive to dry. Cover the patch with wax paper and a couple of books. Let the adhesive dry overnight.

# HOW TO REPAIR A SMALL HOLE

**1** Repair small holes with wood putty. Use putty that matches the floor color. Force the compound into the hole with a putty knife. Continue to press the putty in this fashion until the depression in the floor is filled. Scrape excess compound from the area. Use a damp, lint-free cloth while the putty is still wet to smooth the top level with the surrounding floor. Allow to dry.

**2** Sand the area with fine (100- to 120-grit) sandpaper. Sand with the wood grain so the splintered area is flush with the surrounding surface. To better hide the repair, feather sand the area. Wipe up dust with a slightly damp cloth.

**3** With a clean, lint-free cloth, apply a matching stain (wood sealer or "restorer") to the sanded area. Read the label on the product to make sure it is appropriate for sealing wood floors. Work in the stain until the patched area blends with the rest of the floor. Allow area to completely dry. Apply two coats of finish. Be sure the finish is the same as that which was used on the surrounding floor.

## HERE'S HOW

Surface finish (poly or wax)

Penetrant finish

**Wax finish**

To determine what kind of surface you have, use a coin to lightly scrape the floor in a hidden corner. If flakes appear, you have either a surface finish or a wax coat. If no flakes appear, it's a penetrant. To check for wax, sprinkle water on the floor. If the beads turn white after 10 minutes, it's waxed.

# Repairing Springy Floors

## 5

Joists without adequate bridging or "X-bracing" can move or twist or bounce, leaving the boards off-center. Adding adequate joist bridging cuts deflection by about 50 percent. Bridging allows a joist to transfer the weight it supports to neighboring joists.

A BOUNCY FLOOR IS OFTEN JUST A DEFLECTION ISSUE (HOW MUCH THE JOISTS flex), which is fairly easy to fix. It's important to address the issue, for a springy floor may result in cracked drywall. In new houses, where the wood is still relatively new and moist, the deflection issues may go away on their own as the wood dries and stiffens. If your floors are sagging, it is likely you are dealing with a structural issue (how strong the joists are across a span). In the latter case, you need to install a supporting wall or beam to shorten the span of each joist. Before you start working, call up your local building inspection office to tell them what you plan to do. Often this call comes with free advice from a local inspector.

# FLOOR BRACING 101

## TOOLS & SUPPLIES YOU NEED

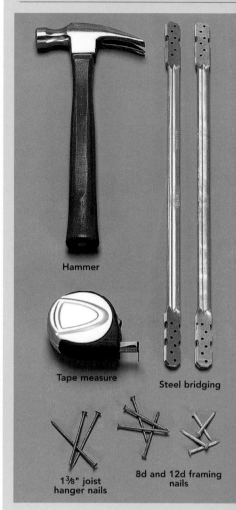

Hammer

Tape measure

Steel bridging

1⅜" joist hanger nails

8d and 12d framing nails

There should be very little bounciness near the exterior of the house, where the joists are supported by the foundation. Similarly, there should be very little bounciness directly above the place where the joists are supported by a beam (usually the center of a long room). If the bounciness is just as severe directly over the center beam as it is above other parts of the joist, the beam below is either undersized or not supported sufficiently by posts. It may be a good idea to call up a professional to help with this.

## SKILLS YOU NEED

• Hammering
• Measuring

## TERMS YOU NEED TO KNOW

SUBFLOOR—The base layer of wood or plywood that supports the underlayment and surface flooring.

UNDERLAYMENT—The intermediate layer between the surface flooring material and the subfloor. The underlayment for laminate flooring combines a poly-water barrier and a foam cushion sound barrier in a rollout or rigid-plank form.

JOISTS—Supporting beams set parallel from wall to wall to support the subfloor.

## DIFFICULTY LEVEL

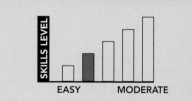

EASY        MODERATE

This project can be completed in as little as 30 minutes.

## TERMS YOU NEED TO KNOW

JOISTS—Supporting beams set parallel from wall to wall to support the subfloor.

JOIST BRIDGING—Wood or metal bracing that is placed between joists at mid-span to prevent the joists from twisting and to more evenly distribute the weight supported by the bridged joists.

BEAM—A beefy horizontal framing member that runs perpendicular to the joists, usually near the middle of a long joist span, to help bear the weight placed on the joists.

DEFLECTION—How much the joists flex.

SPAN—The horizontal distance between two vertical supports. The span of a joist is the horizontal distance between the wall and the opposite wall, or between the wall and the next supporting post or beam.

X-BRACING—Wood or metal bridging that is diagonally inserted between two floor joists. The two braces together look like an X when viewed from the side.

SOLID BRIDGING—A solid piece of wood, usually the same width as the joists, that is inserted between two floor joists to bridge the joists.

**1** Measure the distance from the center of the width of one joist to the center of the width of the neighboring joist. Home centers carry metal bridging to fit between joists that are centered 16" or 24" apart.

**2** Measure the length of the joist span in feet. Have someone help you by holding the tape against one wall while you measure to the opposing wall. Divide this number by 3—the amount of feet from each foundation wall you should begin your first row of metal bridging. For example, if your joists span 9 ft., place bridging 3 ft. from each foundation wall. Install a row in the center of the span, too (4½ ft. from each wall, in this case), if there's not already one there.

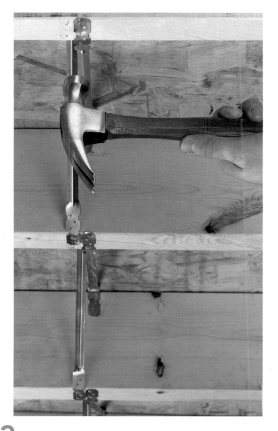

**3** Fasten metal bridging with 1⅜" joist hanger nails. Each piece of bridging requires four nails, two at each end. You're done!

## SHOPPING TIP

Metal and steel bracing are available in standard sizes at most home centers. Metal bracing may be added to the underside of a floor that has existing wood bracing.

## HERE'S HOW

Check the strength and overall condition of the original bridging. If any of it is loose, secure the edges of the bridging to the joists by adding some nails. Use 1⅜" joist hanger nails for metal bridging and 8- or 12-penny framing nails for wood bridging. After securing the existing bridging to the joists, add X-bracing where needed.

# Fixing Squeaky Floors
## from Below

6

Squeak-elimination tools, such as the Squeak-Ender (shown), tighten the joist to the subfloor and eliminate squeaks. See page 38 for instructions.

LOTS OF HOUSES SQUEAK, SO MOST OF US JUST ACCEPT IT AS A FACT OF LIFE. It doesn't have to be, though. With a little work, you can get rid of those pesky squeaks. The cause of a floor talking back to you is no mystery; it's just the sound of wood rubbing against a nail or another piece of wood. More often than not the squeaking is just caused by the wood expanding due to humidity, contracting due to dryness. Wood is a very porous material. It just does that.

So how do we make it stop? If you have access to the area below the squeaky floor (as is the case if the immediate level below has an unfinished ceiling), please read on. . . .

# FLOOR SQUEAKS 101

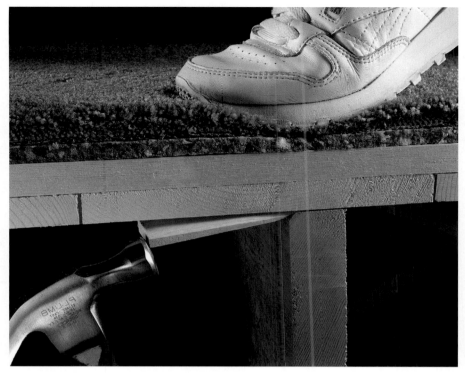

Hammer

Flashlight

Electric drill

Masking tape

Squeak-elimination tool, such as the Squeak-Ender

Folding ruler

Wood glue

#8 drill bit

¾" spade bit

#10 flat-head wood screws

Wrench

Washers

Wood shims

#10 drill bit

Phillips screwdriver

To pinpoint the source of a squeak, have someone walk around upstairs while you're below the floor (on the lower level). Make a pencil mark on the unfinished ceiling where you hear the offending chirp or squawk. The subfloor may even visually move away from the joists when you hear the squeak. If you don't see any movement, the finished flooring has buckled up away from the subfloor. If this is the case, have the person upstairs place a heavy weight, such as a couch leg or cinder block, on the spot that squeaks. If the squeak is immediately over a joist, use a hammer to tap a wood shim in between the joist and subfloor. Directions to do so are given in this project (starting on the next page).

## SKILLS YOU NEED

- Drilling
- Hammering
- Wrench and screwdriver work

## DIFFICULTY LEVEL

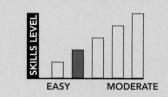

EASY          MODERATE

This project can be completed in as little as 10 minutes or as much as 2 hours.

## TERMS YOU NEED TO KNOW

SUBFLOOR—The base layer of wood or plywood that supports the underlayment and surface flooring.

UNDERLAYMENT—The intermediate layer between the surface flooring material and the subfloor. The underlayment for laminate flooring combines a poly-water barrier and a foam cushion sound barrier in a rollout or rigid-plank form.

JOISTS—Supporting beams set parallel from wall to wall to support the subfloor.

SQUEAK-ENDER FLOOR SQUEAK ELIMINATOR—A commercial squeak-elimination tool. It consists of a threaded rod attached to a flat mounting plate and a steel bracket fitted with a squared-off hook on one end.

**1** If there is a gap or movement between the subfloor and joist at the squeak location, tap a tapered wood shim into the gap. First smear it with construction adhesive or wood glue. Squirt some glue into the gap, too. Don't overtap; it makes the gap bigger. Wait for the glue to dry. If this doesn't stop the squeak, go to Step 2.

**2** To use a Squeak-Ender, or another comparable squeak-elimination tool, insert the head of the hanger bolt into the concave part of the anchor plate. Use a Phillips screwdriver to screw the mounting plate to the underside of the subfloor (four screws are often provided). You want the plate to be touching the nearest joist in the general area of the squeak.

**3** Slide the top part of the joist bracket through the threaded hanger rod and the bottom part under the joist.

**4** Slip the washer and hex nut onto the rod. With a wrench, tighten the nut until the subfloor is pulled snug against the joist. Avoid overtightening.

## TOOL TIP

The Squeak-Ender set may not come with a lock washer, but a lock washer prevents the nut from loosening.

**1** If you've made it this far, the squeak is not caused by a gap between the subfloor and the joist. It's likely the floorboards have buckled up, creating a gap between the floor and the subfloor. We're going to drill up through the subfloor and pull the flooring down tight against the subfloor with some wood screws. To figure out how long the screws should be, first determine the combined thickness of the floor and subfloor by measuring at existing cutouts in the floor. NOTE: The subfloor is usually ¾".

### WHAT IF . . . ?

If there are no cutouts, determine the thickness by carefully boring a hole up into the subfloor. The hole should be large enough to fit a tape measure into it. Just to be safe, work in an inconspicuous corner of the basement. Use a ¾" spade drill bit to drill up into the subfloor. Stop drilling every so often to see how close to the finish floor you are—you may need a flashlight to see clearly. Stop once you get to the finish floor. Measure. Do not drill all the way through your wood floor above.

To find out the thickness of the top floor, measure the depth of the floor on the first stair down to the basement, if you have one.

**2** Drill pilot holes. The length of screw we need is ¼" less than the total depth of the top floor and subfloor combined. Mark that depth with masking tape on a #8 wood drill bit. On a #10 drill bit, mark the depth of the subfloor only. Now, drill some pilot holes around the squeak: 1. Drill through the subfloor with the thicker #10 bit. 2. Drill into the same holes a little deeper with the #8 bit. Make sure you don't drill deeper than the masking tape marks.

### HERE'S HOW

The length of screw we need for Step 2 is the same length we marked on the #8 drill bit. The thread thickness, though, is going to be a #10. This way, as the screw is tightened, the hole left in the subfloor by the #10 drill bit will not offer any resistance, but the hole left in the top flooring with the #8 drill bit will be snug and pull the loose board down against the subfloor. To distribute the pressure around the screw, slip each screw through a large fender washer before driving the screws into each pilot hole. This will secure the subfloor to the wood floor and stop the squeak.

# Fixing Squeaky Floors from Above

**7**

It's a little more work to fix squeaks from above the floorboards than from below, but it's a lot easier than you might think.

THE SOUND OF WOOD RUBBING ON WOOD OR AGAINST A NAIL CAN BE infuriating, but fortunately this problem is not too complicated to fix. If the ceiling below the squeaky floor is unfinished, you can go downstairs and actually watch for movement in the subfloor while someone else walks on the floor upstairs. If you can't get to the floor from below, you have to fix the squeak from above. This is done by setting loose boards or surface nailing them down. Alternatively, a squeak-ender designed specifically for above floors may be used.

There are a few key topics discussed in this section. Learn how to:

- Apply lubricants to the floorboards to eliminate subtle squeaks caused by dryness.

- Safely use a hammer to tap loose floorboards into place.

- Carefully drill a small hole through the surface of the floor to surface-nail gaps, and then hide the evidence. Let's get started.

# SQUEAK ELIMINATION 101

There are squeak-elimination tools for working above and below the floor. Even if your floor is carpeted, a squeak-elimination tool can drive screws through the subfloor and into the joists for you. The device controls the depth.

Keep in mind, that annoying squeak in your floor is caused by any of four things: 1. two floorboards rubbing together; 2. the subfloor rubbing against the joist below it; 3. the subfloor rubbing against the floorboards above it; 4. a loose nail in any of these places.

## TERMS YOU NEED TO KNOW

SUBFLOOR—The base layer of wood or plywood that supports the underlayment and surface flooring.

JOISTS—Supporting beams set parallel from wall to wall to support the subfloor.

## SKILLS YOU NEED

- Hammering
- Drilling
- Using a putty knife
- Using a nail set

## DIFFICULTY LEVEL

This project can be completed in as little as 10 minutes or as much as 2 hours.

# HOW TO SET LOOSE BOARDS

**B**ecause small squeaks can be caused by dirt between floorboards or by dryness, clean the floor at least once a week and  apply lubricants to areas that tend to be extra dry or squeaky.

Oils: graphite, mineral oil, or floor oil. Use powdered or liquid graphite sparingly; it can make a mess. Similarly, a few drops of mineral oil will do the trick, but using too much can stain the surface. Floor oil, applied generously into the joints, soaks into the wood, making it expand. This results in a snug tongue-and-groove fitting. That pesky squeak may just disappear at this stage, at least temporarily.

Powders: graphite and talcum powder. To use talcum powder, dust a generous amount of the powder wherever the floor makes noise. Use a dry, clean cloth to work it into the tongue-and-groove joints, especially near any visible nails. Slightly dampen the cloth with water to wipe away excess powder.

**2** Place the 2 × 4 at right angles to the squeaky floorboards. Tap the 2 × 4 with a hammer to reseat any loose boards or nails. Start at the perimeter of the squeaky section, moving the 2 × 4 in a rectangular pattern until you get to the center.

**1** Make a "beater" block. If loose nails are the problem, you can tap the floorboards down where you hear the squeak. Wrap a 2 × 4 scrap (length of 1 ft. should do) in a heavy towel or scrap of carpet so that you don't scratch the floor surface. Tack the carpet to the top of the 2 × 4 with nails.

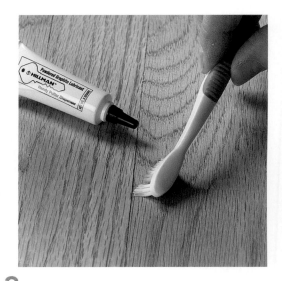

**3** Squeaks in hardwood floors caused by floorboards rubbing against each other or against a nail can sometimes be eliminated for a few weeks or months just by adding a hardwood floor lubricant at the point of friction. First remove dirt and debris from between the floorboards, using an old toothbrush. With a clean toothbrush or a clean cloth, apply the lubricant to the floor joints.

**1** As a last resort, reattach buckled floorboards to the subfloor by nailing them down (from above the floorboards) with flooring nails. To reduce the risk of the boards splitting, drill pilot holes slightly smaller than the diameter of the nails. For maximum holding power, drill at opposing angles in a staggered pattern every 4" to 6" along the squeaky boards. The goal is to drill through the surface flooring of the buckled board and into the subfloor; better yet, drill into the subfloor and a joist.

**2** Set the nails with a nail set.

**3** Fill nail holes with wood putty, using a putty knife. Force the compound into the hole by pressing the knife blade downward until it lies flat on the floor. Allow the patch to dry completely.

---

### HERE'S HOW

**LOCATE JOISTS** Not all of the nails can hit a joist, but you get a stronger connection wherever they do. Use a stud finder to find the joists.

**COUNTERSINK NAILS** Hide the head of the nails beneath the surface of the wood by gently tapping the nails down with a nail set. This is called "countersinking" the nails. Fill nail holes with tinted putty. Use a slightly damp sponge to smooth excess putty.

**PROTECT YOUR FLOOR FROM DENTS** Before tapping nails into your pre-drilled holes, cut out small squares of cardboard to set around the nailing area. It's a good idea to use a smooth-faced hammer as well.

**REMOVE DENTS** Some hammer dents can be removed by placing a damp cloth on the spot and applying pressure with a hot iron. This raises the damaged surface back to the common surface.

**4** Sand the patch flush with the surrounding surface. Use fine-grit sandpaper and sand in the direction of the wood grain. Apply wood restorer to the area (inset) until it blends with the surrounding floor.

# Repairing Resilient Flooring

## 8

Air pockets and curls are unsightly and they only get worse over time. Curls invite debris and moisture to settle under the tile, thus weakening the surrounding tiles; and bubbles continue to swell, destroying the adhesive holding the sheet of flooring in place. These problems must be addressed immediately.

RESILIENT FLOORING IS DURABLE, BUT FROM TIME TO TIME MINOR REPAIRS must be addressed. Air pockets are caused by the adhesive no longer working. This is common as floors age, and the resulting bubble is fairly easy to deflate and rebond to the subfloor. If not attended to, the area will eventually harden, split, and crack—making the problem more noticeable and difficult to fix. Even a curled edge on an otherwise healthy vinyl tile can be easily glued back into place. If the repair doesn't hold, the entire tile must be replaced (see page 48).

# RESILIENT CONSTRUCTION 101

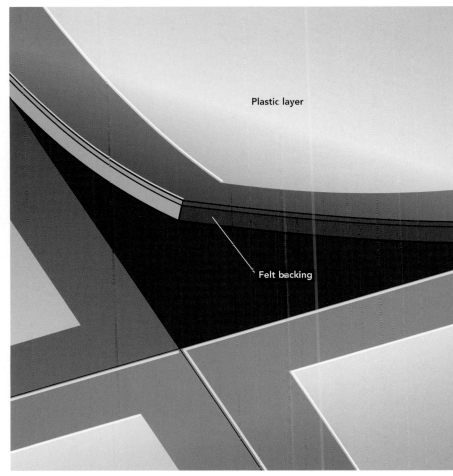

Plastic layer

Felt backing

The reason vinyl tiles curl is due to their construction. Vinyl of any kind is made with plastics. Over time the plastic layer shrinks, but the felt backing does not. As a result, tiles have gaps between them and the edges curl.

## TERMS YOU NEED TO KNOW

J-ROLLER—A small handheld rubber roller used to apply even pressure over small areas of flooring to help the adhesive bond to the underlayment.

LIQUID SEAM SEALER—A clear compound that permanently bonds, fuses, or seals cuts and seams in resilient flooring.

MASTIC—A thick sealant or adhesive with putty-like properties that is usually tar based.

## TOOLS & SUPPLIES YOU NEED

Mineral spirits

Heat gun

Vinyl adhesive

Utility knife

Putty knife

Liquid seam sealer

J-roller

Old Toothbrush

Damp cloth

Wax paper    Soapy water

Toothpicks

## SKILLS YOU NEED

- Cutting with a utility knife
- Applying glue with a flexible tool
- Using a heat gun
- Applying seam sealer

## DIFFICULTY LEVEL

SKILLS LEVEL

EASY    MODERATE

This project can be completed in 30 minutes, not including drying time.

**1** Deflate air pocket. Use a utility knife to lightly score and then slice through the bulge. This allows air to escape. Extend the cut a little (½") beyond the blister at both ends. If possible, cut along a line in the pattern to hide the cut.

**2** Choose an appropriately sized tool to force fresh vinyl adhesive through the slit and under the bubble. Press the edges together. Wipe up any excess adhesive with a damp cloth.

**3** Let the adhesive dry. Cover the patch with wax paper and some books overnight.

### WHAT IF . . . ?

If you have a small tear in the flooring, some debris may have accumulated in the crack. Use a vacuum to remove debris and clean out chunks with a toothpick, utility knife, putty knife, or an old toothbrush. Dipping a toothbrush in diluted ammonia helps raise sticky parts.

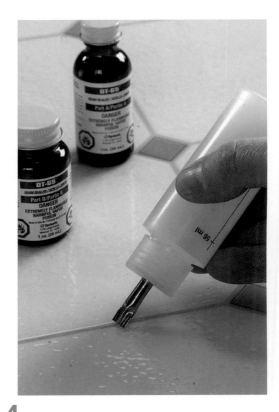

**4** To hide the seam, purchase a liquid seam sealer kit and mix the ingredients according to the manufacturer's instructions. Using an applicator bottle, squeeze a thin bead of the mixture onto the cut. Allow the sealer to dry.

**1** If the corner or edge of vinyl tile is curling, but the rest of the tile is in good shape, you can refasten it. Use an electric heat gun to warm the area. This makes the vinyl easier to work with and it softens the underlying adhesive.

**2** If you cannot refasten the tile as is, first vacuum up debris. To clean sticky areas, use a toothpick or old toothbrush dipped in soapy water or diluted ammonia. Dissolve old adhesive with mineral spirits. Use liquids minimally to avoid loosening adjacent tiles. Allow to dry.

**3** Use a flexible tool (such as a small putty knife) to lift the tile just enough to spread the underside with fresh adhesive. Wipe up excess glue with a damp cloth or sponge.

**4** Press the curled edge into place. If necessary, apply pressure with a J-roller or rolling pin to create a solid bond. Start at the center and work toward the edge, working out all air bubbles. Wipe up excess glue with a damp cloth.

### SAFETY FIRST

Do not under any circumstances use the heat gun after applying highly flammable solvents.

### WHAT IF . . . ?

If one edge overlaps the other because the flooring has stretched, put the short end over the longer end and use it as a guide to trim the longer piece with a utility knife. Remove the trimmed-off scrap.

## 9

# Replacing Resilient Tiles

Even the smallest of tears can leave an unsightly blemish on vinyl tiles.
Deep scratches can allow moisture under the tile and loosen the adhesive,
so it's necessary to replace the entire tile.

RESILIENT TILES ARE SUBJECT TO BEING TORN, DENTED, GOUGED, PUNCTURED, or burned. The beautiful thing about vinyl tiles is that they are easy to replace. To replace dry-back resilient tiles you must take the time to thoroughly remove old adhesive from the subfloor, clean the vacant spot on the floor, and then lay an even layer of new adhesive to ensure the new tile sits flush with the rest of the floor. Removing sticky-back tiles requires a little more work up front to scrape up the damaged tile, but laying the new tile is a breeze thanks to the self-adhesive backing.

# RESILIENT TILE REMOVAL 101

It's important to thoroughly dissolve old adhesive with a stain-removing solution and to scrape the subfloor clean with a putty knife. Even the most insignificant bits and pieces of debris can create noticeable bumps. Beyond cosmetic considerations, foreign matter trapped under a vinyl tile weakens the adhesive. In some cases, debris may even cause the tile to crack.

## TERMS YOU NEED TO KNOW

UNDERLAYMENT—The intermediate layer between the surface flooring material and the subfloor. The underlayment for resilient flooring is oftentimes a ¼"-thick piece of plywood installed to provide a smooth, even surface for a new floor.

TROWEL—A flat-blade hand tool with a raised handle used for scooping, spreading, leveling, smoothing, or shaping substances such as cement, mortar, or adhesive. Usually, a tile trowel has notches on one edge for combing mortar or adhesive into even rows.

J-ROLLER—A small handheld rubber roller used to apply even pressure over small areas of flooring, which helps the adhesive bond to the underlayment.

## TOOLS & SUPPLIES YOU NEED

Vinyl tile adhesive · Spray bottle · Stain-removing solutions · Replacement tiles · Asbestos-rated respirator · Clean cloth · Wax paper · Heat gun · Flat, heavy objects · Floor scraper · Vacuum · Putty knife · Utility knife · J-roller · ⅛" notched trowel

## SKILLS YOU NEED

- Scraping
- Vacuuming
- Simple trowel work
- Using a heat gun

## DIFFICULTY LEVEL

SKILLS LEVEL

EASY     MODERATE

This project can be completed in 1 hour, not including drying time.

## GETTING STARTED

If you do not have any extra tiles, you have these three basic options.

1. If you're lucky, the floor won't be too old and you can find some matching tiles at a flooring store. It's a good idea to bring a photograph or sample of the floor so you can get an exact match. And if you find one, buy some extra tiles in case you need them in the future.

2. If your tiles cannot be found at flooring outlets, you may also try taking a tile from under an appliance, from the back of a closet, or from an inconspicuous corner. Use it for the repair, and fill the empty square with a new tile that closely matches the old tiles, as close as possible given the available options.

3. As a last resort, consider using a patterned tile of the same size that harmonizes with the ones you have. There are many decorative touches to make this work. For example, you could replace a few additional tiles along with the damaged one to give your floor a unique inset pattern.

---

**SAFETY FIRST**

Resilient tile installed before 1986 could have asbestos backing. Asbestos fibers are only dangerous when they are airborne. Mist the area with a spray bottle to keep the area moist. Just to be extra safe, wear an asbestos-rated respirator. You can find an inexpensive one at most home centers. Note: Asbestos will go right through a simple dust mask. If you want to be sure you are properly protected, you can take a sample of the asbestos to your local Environmental Protection Agency or your state health department.

---

**1** Use an electric heat gun to warm the damaged tile and soften the underlying adhesive. Keep the heat source moving so you don't melt the tile. When an edge of the tile begins to curl, insert a putty knife to pry up the loose edge until you can remove the tile. NOTE: If you can clearly see the seam between tiles, first score around the tile with a utility knife. This prevents other tiles from lifting.

**2** Scrape away remaining adhesive with a putty knife or, for stubborn spots, a floor scraper. Work from the edges to the center so that you don't accidentally scrape up the adjacent tiles. Use mineral spirits to dissolve leftover goop. Take care not to allow the mineral spirits to soak into the floor under adjacent tiles. Continue to use a sharp floor scraper to scrape to the bare wood underlayment. Use a damp cloth to wipe up the mess. Vacuum up dust, dirt, and adhesive. Wipe clean.

**3** When the floor is dry, use a notched trowel—with ⅛" V-shaped notches—held at a 45° angle to apply a thin, even layer of vinyl tile adhesive onto the underlayment. **NOTE:** Only follow this step if you have dry-back tiles.

**4** Set one edge of the tile in place. Lower the tile onto the underlayment and then press it into place. Apply pressure with a J-roller to create a solid bond, starting at the center and working toward the edge to work out air bubbles. If adhesive oozes out the sides, wipe it up with a damp cloth or sponge.

**5** Let adhesive dry for 24 hours. Cover the tile with wax paper and some books.

# Patching Resilient Sheet Flooring

## 10

Resilient flooring is vulnerable when it comes to extreme heat and heavy objects falling on it. Burn marks and dents can be fixed by cutting out the damaged section and replacing it with a new patch of matching flooring.

RESILIENT SHEET FLOORING IS A DURABLE, PRACTICAL MATERIAL. There are no seams, so it is impervious to spills. However, it is not impervious to tears, dents, gouges, punctures, or burns. To repair a damaged section of sheet flooring, cut out the damaged area and glue in a replacement patch from a leftover remnant. If you don't have any leftover pieces available, you could settle for a close match or choose a piece that offers an interesting contrast.

# SHEET VINYL PATCHES 101

Remember to thoroughly sweep and vacuum underlayment before installing a vinyl patch. Sometimes the tiniest bits and pieces of debris create noticeable bumps. And if old adhesive is not completely removed, a yellow discoloration will form on your new patch.

## TERMS YOU NEED TO KNOW

UNDERLAYMENT—The intermediate layer between the surface flooring material and the subfloor.

PERIMETER-INSTALL—Vinyl sheet flooring that is glued only around the edges.

TROWEL—A flat-blade hand tool with a raised handle used for scooping, spreading, leveling, smoothing, or shaping substances such as cement, mortar, or adhesive. Usually, a tile trowel has notches on one edge for combing mortar or adhesive into even rows.

## TOOLS & SUPPLIES YOU NEED

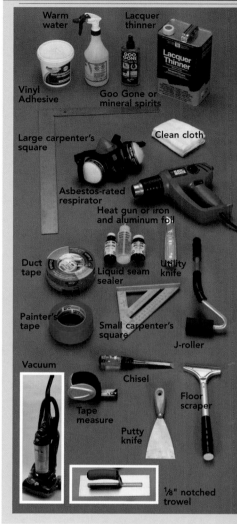

Warm water
Lacquer thinner
Vinyl Adhesive
Goo Gone or mineral spirits
Large carpenter's square
Clean cloth
Asbestos-rated respirator
Heat gun or iron and aluminum foil
Duct tape
Liquid seam sealer
Utility knife
Painter's tape
Small carpenter's square
J-roller
Vacuum
Chisel
Floor scraper
Tape measure
Putty knife
⅛" notched trowel

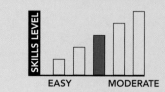

## SKILLS YOU NEED

- Measuring
- Cutting
- Scraping
- Vacuuming
- Simple trowel work

## DIFFICULTY LEVEL

EASY        MODERATE

This project can be completed in 1 hour, not including drying time.

**1** Measure the width and length of the damaged area. Place the new flooring remnant on a surface you don't mind making some cuts on—like a scrap of plywood. Use a carpenter's square for cutting guidance. Make sure your cutting size is a bit larger than the damaged area.

**2** Lay the patch over the damaged area, matching pattern lines. Secure the patch with duct tape. Using a carpenter's square as a cutting guide, cut through the new vinyl (on top) and the old vinyl (on bottom). Press firmly with the knife to cut both layers.

**3** Use tape to mark one edge of the new patch with the corresponding edge of the old flooring as placement marks. Remove the tape around the perimeter of the patch and lift up.

**4** Soften the underlying adhesive with an electric heat gun and remove the damaged section of floor. Work from edges in. When the tile is loosened, insert a putty knife and pry up the damaged area.

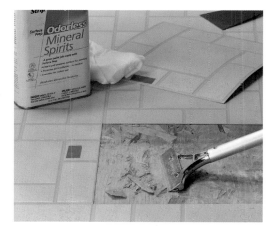

**5** Scrape off the remaining adhesive with a putty knife or chisel. Work from the edges to the center. Dab mineral spirits (or Goo Gone) or spritz warm water on the floor to dissolve leftover goop, taking care not to use too much; you don't want to loosen the surrounding flooring. Use a razor-edged scraper (flooring scraper) to scrape to the bare wood underlayment.

**6** Apply adhesive to the patch, using a notched trowel (with ⅛" V-shaped notches) held at a 45° angle to the back of the new vinyl patch.

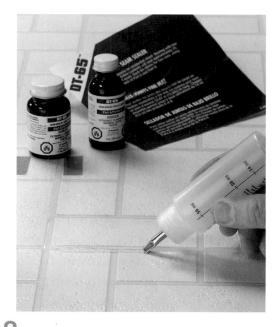

**7** Set one edge of the patch in place. Lower the patch onto the underlayment. Press into place. Apply pressure with a J-roller or rolling pin to create a solid bond. Start at the center and work toward the edges, working out air bubbles. Wipe up adhesive that oozes out the sides with a clean, damp cloth or sponge.

**8** Let the adhesive dry overnight. The next day, hide the seams with liquid seam sealer. Use a soft cloth dipped in lacquer thinner to clean the area. Mix the seam sealer according to the manufacturer's directions. Use an applicator bottle to apply a thin bead of sealer onto the cutlines.

## 11

# Patching Minor Carpet Damage

To create a patch for a small damaged area of carpet, use a template cut out of wood. The template allows you to cut out both the damaged area as well as the new patch.

A SMALL STAIN OR BURN CAN BE CUT OUT OF YOUR CARPET AND PATCHED with a clean carpet remnant. If minor carpet damage is not addressed it can lead to bigger problems. Stains and burns, for example, can attract dirt and grime, making the minor damage worse and even allowing it to spread. If you don't have a remnant piece, you still have a couple of options. If the carpet isn't too old, you may be able to find a matching remnant at a carpet dealer. If not, consider cutting a piece from the back of a closet or from under a couch that you don't intend to move. Due to differences in fading and wear, it's likely the replacement patch will not be perfect. You'll still be able to see the patch, but guests who don't know where to look probably won't see anything.

# CARPET CONSTRUCTION 101

When setting a new patch, tape a piece of burlap to the foam carpet pad and glue the patch to the burlap. The burlap prevents the foam pad from tearing in the event that you need to pull the patch up in the future. Also, if you cut into the carpet pad when cutting out the damaged section of carpet, mend the cut with duct tape.

## TERMS YOU NEED TO KNOW

ROWS OF PILE—Pile (also called "nap") is the carpet surface. It is composed of cut or looped tufts of yarn, woven into the back of the carpet.

CUT-PILE CARPET—Carpet composed of tufts of yarn that are cut off at the top, as opposed to looped.

## TOOLS & SUPPLIES YOU NEED

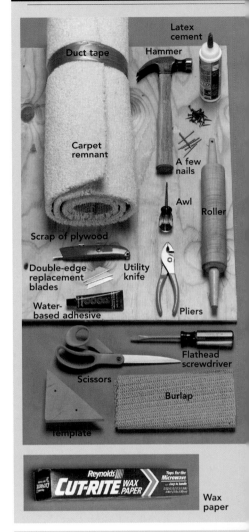

## SKILLS YOU NEED

- Light hammering
- Cutting with a utility knife
- Gluing
- Cutting with scissors

## DIFFICULTY LEVEL

This project can be completed in 30 minutes, not including drying time for the adhesive.

# HOW TO PATCH MINOR CARPET DAMAGE

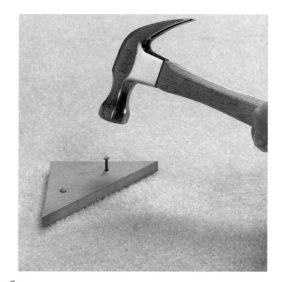

**1** Nail your template over the damaged area and into the floor to keep the template in place as you work. The nails are temporary, so only hammer them in as far as necessary to hold the template in place.

**2** Use a utility knife to cut out the damaged carpet piece. The goal is to cut the carpet backing only. Use the hammer to pry up the nails holding down the template, and set the template aside. Pull the damaged carpet up, using your fingers. Inspect the foam pad under the damaged carpet piece. If you accidentally cut into the pad, use duct tape to mend it.

**3** Place a matching carpet remnant onto a scrap of plywood and place the template on top of that. Cut out a patch for the hole in the carpet, using a utility knife. Be sure to match the nap direction on the replacement patch with the nap of the surrounding carpet. Fan the carpet with your hand to see which direction the fibers are woven. Position the patch in the cutout area in the carpet to make sure it fits snugly.

### HERE'S HOW

To ensure the nap of the patch is aligned with the nap of the surrounding carpet, use a marker to draw arrows on pieces of tape. Use the tape to mark the direction of the nap.

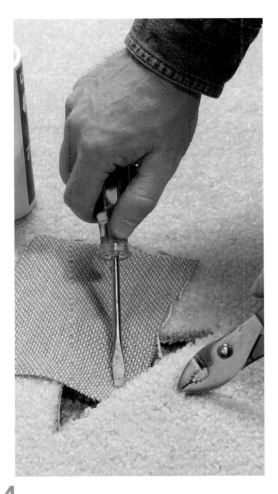

**5** Apply latex cement (or a flexible, water-based adhesive) to the burlap and to the edges of the cutout in the carpet. Use an old screwdriver (or toothpick or even a small flexible knife) to push some glue under the edges of the carpet.

**4** Cut a piece of burlap 1" to 2" larger than the hole, using scissors. To separate the carpet from the carpet pad, grip the surrounding fibers with pliers and lift up. Use a flathead screwdriver to center the fabric under the hole. Secure the burlap to the padding with duct tape.

### WHAT IF . . . ?

If glue oozes out from under your patch, blot it up with a damp, warm sponge while it's still wet. Use a dry towel to blot the wet area, soaking up the leftover glue. If the glue is stubborn or already soaking into the carpet, soak a rag in warm vinegar and lay it over the stain for 30 minutes. Wipe the area clean with a towel. Use a damp sponge to blot up the vinegar.

**6** Check the nap position and then set the patch into the adhesive. Apply light circular pressure with your hand, and then roll over the patch with a rolling pin to evenly distribute pressure. Be sure not to press too hard, and immediately clean up glue that squeezes up onto your carpet. Use an awl to free tufts or loops of pile in the seam. Cover the patch with wax paper and a light stack of books. Let it dry for at least 48 hours.

Sliding furniture across the floor can catch loose carpet seams and further pull them away from the seam tape, leaving a big gap to invite dust and other debris under your carpet. To avoid further problems down the road, fix loose carpet seams immediately—and always lift furniture, instead of sliding it.

SEAM PROBLEMS CAN BE CAUSED BY A SNAG, HEAVY FOOT TRAFFIC, POOR quality, longterm wear, or improper installation. Whatever the cause, if the seams of your wall-to-wall carpet have begun to come apart, fix them as soon as you can. The longer you wait, the more likely your carpet is to fray and the more likely debris will start to accumulate under the carpet. The good news is that the repair requires only minimal skills and simple tools that you can rent at any carpet dealership. Read on . . . you can definitely solve the problem yourself.

# CARPET SEAMS 101

Hardwood floor

Carpet pad

Hot-melt seam tape

Subfloor

Carpet seams are held down with seam tape laid over the foam carpet pad. The tape sticks to the underside of the carpet. If the carpet is set onto the seam tape crookedly, it will leave a noticeable gap. In this case, the tape should be removed, and the seams should be reset.

## TOOLS & SUPPLIES YOU NEED

Seam iron

Hot-melt seam tape

Heavy-duty work gloves

Carpet roller

Sharp scissors

Tape measure

Utility knife

Razor blades

## SKILLS YOU NEED

- Measuring
- Cutting
- Using a seam iron
- Using a small carpet roller

## DIFFICULTY LEVEL

SKILLSLEVEL

EASY        MODERATE

This project can be completed in under an hour.

**1** Separate the carpet fibers along the seam with your fingers, so you can clearly see the seam. Use a carpet or utility knife to cut through the seam tape stuck to the underside of the carpet. Open up the entire length of the seam and remove any remaining tape. Be careful not to cut the carpet pad. If you cut the pad, repair it with duct tape.

**2** If there are any loose carpet fibers that could accidentally be pulled, snip them close to the base of the carpet.

**3** Measure the length of the split seam and cut a new piece of hot-melt seam tape to size. Hold back one edge of carpet (not the carpet pad) while you slip the seam tape, adhesive side up, under the seam. Center the tape between the two pieces of carpet.

### SAFETY FIRST

**B**e sure to regularly replace the blades in your utility knife. A dull utility knife requires you to use more pressure, which makes accurate cutting more difficult.

**4** Place the seam iron on a board or old carpet remnant and pre-heat it to the appropriate temperature, as recommended by the seam-tape manufacturer (usually 250°).

**5** Hold back one side of the carpet and place the hot iron directly on the tape at one end of the seam. Hold it there for about 30 seconds, so that it melts the tape glue. Let the carpet flop down over the iron and slowly draw the iron along the entire length of the seam. Go about a foot at a time. Check to make sure the carpet is not too hot and then press the carpet down into the heated adhesive with the other hand. As you go, make sure the backings are butted together. The glue will harden in just a couple of minutes.

**6** Set the carpet to the seam tape by walking over the seam. Alternatively, roll over the seam with a handheld, spiked seam roller (available at most home-improvement stores).

**HERE'S HOW**

To ensure that the carpet will not fray at the seams, apply a continuous bead of seam glue along the seam edges.

## 13

# Repairing Concrete Cracks

Although concrete is a very durable substance, it can still be chipped by heavy objects or cracked due to abrupt changes in temperature or the house shifting.

CRACKS, CHIPS, AND FLAKING SURFACES ARE NOT ONLY UGLY, BUT THEY CAUSE the surrounding areas to deteriorate, turning a simple repair into a major project. It's best to patch and repair damaged concrete as soon as possible. Since there are a variety of repair compounds on the market, research which product is best suited for the job. Some are better for general patching while others are good for cracks and fractures; some are suited for large areas while others are best for small repairs.

When patching concrete it's important to clean first. Concrete is formed by a chemical reaction between portland cement and water, which is called "hydration." The interaction creates tiny crystals that interlock with one another, binding the sand and gravel aggregates into its structure. If there's dirt in the repair, the crystals bond to the dirt instead of the old concrete and the repair flakes out over time. So long as the cleaning steps in this project are taken seriously, the repairs are strong and long-lasting.

# CONCRETE REPAIR 101

Concrete is composed of coarse and fine aggregates (sand and gravel), portland cement, and water. Portland cement chemically reacts with water to create a sticky paste. This coats the aggregates and then hardens into the rock-hard mass that we call concrete. Concrete-repair caulks and vinyl-repair material are as plastic and malleable as newly mixed cement and about as strong and durable when hardened, but it fits into tighter cracks and chips than a cement-based repair compound.

## TERMS YOU NEED TO KNOW

BACK-CHISEL—Tilt the chisel back toward you when chiseling around the edges of a hole in concrete, so that the base of the hole is wider than the top (like a pyramid). A large base of concrete then supports a small top portion rather than the other way around. Also called "keying."

TROWEL—A flat-blade hand tool with a raised handle used for scooping, spreading, leveling, smoothing, or shaping cement or mortar. A steel trowel used for cement has smooth edges and may be either rectangular or oval.

## TOOLS & SUPPLIES YOU NEED

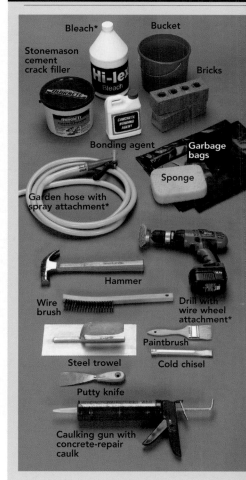

Bleach*
Bucket
Stonemason cement crack filler
Bricks
Bonding agent
Garbage bags
Sponge
Garden hose with spray attachment*
Hammer
Wire brush
Drill with wire wheel attachment*
Paintbrush
Steel trowel
Cold chisel
Putty knife
Caulking gun with concrete-repair caulk

* Optional

## SKILLS YOU NEED

- Cleaning
- Simple trowel work
- Mixing concrete patch compound

## DIFFICULTY LEVEL

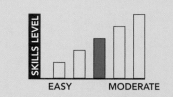

SKILLS LEVEL

EASY          MODERATE

This project can be completed in an hour, not including drying time.

# HOW TO REPAIR CONCRETE CRACKS

**1** Use a concrete chisel (called a "cold chisel") and a heavy hammer or mallet to deepen the edges of the damaged area until the outer edges are at least ⅛" thick. Most cracks and depressions in concrete floors are deeper in the center and are tapered at the edges; the feather thin material around the perimeter of the hole is liable to peel or flake off, which results in an unstable surface for a patch.

**2** Clean out the area to be patched, using a wire brush or portable drill with a wire wheel attachment. Be sure to remove all dirt and loose material from the area to be patched. This step will also roughen the edges a bit, creating a better bond.

## SAFETY FIRST

When doing this kind of work, protect your eyes from chips and particles of cement by wearing eye protection. Also protect your hands from scrapes by wearing work gloves.

## TOOL TIP

Small cracks and fractures ⅛" to ½" wide are often difficult to repair with most cement-based repair compounds because it's just hard to force the mixture into such a narrow opening. However, concrete-repair caulks are perfect for dealing with hairline cracks. Stonemason concrete-repair caulk comes in a tube that fits a caulking gun, so a bead of cement filler can be delivered to the exact area you need to fill.

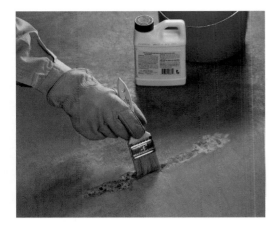

**3** A bonding agent (also called a bonding "adhesive") helps to chemically bond the patch material to the existing concrete, making the repair material less likely to loosen or dislodge. Apply a thin layer of bonding adhesive to the entire repair area with a paintbrush. Some bonding agents need to be applied to a wet surface, others should not. Follow the directions carefully.

**5** Apply a concrete patching compound. Use a trowel to compact the material into the area being repaired. Continue to pack patching compound into the area until it is slightly raised above the surface of the surrounding concrete, approximately $\frac{1}{16}$". For best results, apply the patch in $\frac{1}{4}$"-deep increments. If the hole is deeper than that, allow each layer to dry before applying the next layer. This prevents the top from drying out and shrinking while the lower areas are wet, which could cause recracking.

**4** Mix your concrete patching compound with clean water until all of the material is thoroughly wet and all of the lumps are worked out. The ideal workable consistency for most compounds is like that of very thick gravy. Most mixing compounds will start to set within 10–20 minutes, so only mix a small amount at a time and work fast.

---

**WHAT IF . . . ?**

If mildew, mold, or algae is in the crack or on the surrounding concrete surface near the crack, use a 1:5 solution of bleach and water to remove it. If necessary, use a pressure washer (or garden hose with spray attachment) to remove the remaining mess and small pieces of debris. Allow the area to completely dry.

**6** Use the edge of the trowel to smooth the surface, removing any excess material. Slide the trowel back and forth on its edge, while also pulling the excess material toward you, until it is past the edge of the area you're working on. Scoop it up with the trowel and discard.

**7** Finishing work. Slightly raise the flat face of the steel finishing trowel and smooth the patching material until it is even with the adjoining surfaces, creating a seamless repair. Keep the trowel clean and damp to prevent the mix from gumming up the trowel. Finishing is an art and takes practice, so keep trying. Remember that the patching compound will be easier to work with when it's at a slightly stiff consistency.

**HERE'S HOW**

When working with stonemason concrete-repair caulk, apply no thicker than 3⁄8" caulk at a time. Use a putty knife to press the caulk into the crack and to level the top layer.

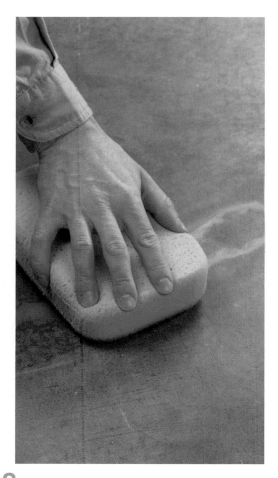

**9** Cover with plastic. Some patch materials suggest that you cover the finished patch with a piece of plastic for a few days. This keeps the moisture from evaporating and gives the cement more time to cure. Make sure to weigh down the edges of the plastic.

**8** Use a slightly damp sponge to smooth out the remaining imperfections and clean off the edges. This actually works wonders and is a great way to compensate for being inexperienced at doing finish work with the trowel.

**TOOL TIP**

For deep repairs, mix in a few nails with the patching material. Essentially, the nails serve the same purpose as the rock aggregate already in a bag of concrete mix; they allow the bonding agent in cement to bond to them. Nails are sometimes useful, though, because they can fit into tighter spaces than gravel, as well as being able to reinforce the strength of the concrete over a larger area than individual rocks.

**10** Smooth. After the compound is cured, you can use the edge of the trowel to scrape the patched areas smooth, if necessary.

# Replacing Ceramic Tiles

## 14

Removing a damaged tile requires a little elbow grease. The first step is to weaken the tile with the appropriate tools (as will be explained in this project). From that point, the job is much easier if you have a large, sturdy chisel to remove chunks of the tile.

A CRACKED OR BROKEN CERAMIC TILE IS EASY ENOUGH TO REPLACE, PROVIDED you have a suitable replacement tile. Before starting this project, shop around a bit for the replacement tile. If you have to buy a new tile, make sure you only look at tile specifically for floors. Take the exact measurement of the broken tile with you. If possible, take a fragment of the tile along with you so the sales person can match the finish and composition. If you absolutely cannot find a replacement tile, consider turning the problem into a design challenge by replacing a few tiles in a pattern of your choice with a contrasting tile. If you need to replace multiple tiles for whatever reason, see page 74 for grouting and sealing large areas.

# CERAMIC TILE MATERIALS 101

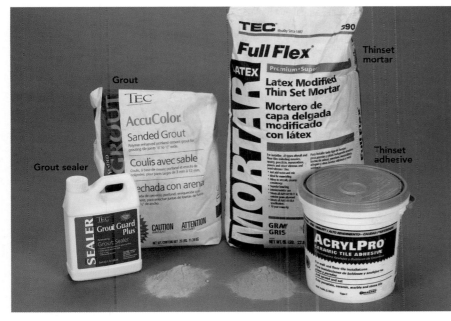

Replacing a tile requires a new tile, adhesive, grout, and a sealer. The joints between ceramic tiles are filled with a cement-based filler called "grout." This must be removed and replaced when a single tile is replaced. It is good to occasionally check the condition of the grout over the entire floor. (To regrout floors, see page 74). Grout is available in tinted colors to match your tile. You must also seal all grout lines with silicone sealer. Seal the joints every two years or so.

## TERMS YOU NEED TO KNOW

SUBFLOOR—The base layer of wood or plywood that supports the underlayment and surface flooring.

UNDERLAYMENT—The intermediate layer between the surface flooring material and the subfloor. The underlayment for a ceramic tile floor can be plywood or cementboard.

THINSET MORTAR—A cement-based adhesive used to adhere ceramic tile to the underlayment.

TILE SPACERS—Small plastic spacers used to position tiles for uniform grout lines. Available in different sizes to create grout joints of different widths.

GROUT—A very fine cement mortar, sometimes tinted, used to fill the joints between ceramic tiles.

METAL LATHE—An open fabric of metal that holds poured mortar used as a base for ceramic tile. You are most likely to see this in older tile installations.

CARBIDE-TIPPED GROUT SAW—A scraping tool with a sharp carbide-coated blade to remove old, hardened grout.

## TOOLS & SUPPLIES YOU NEED

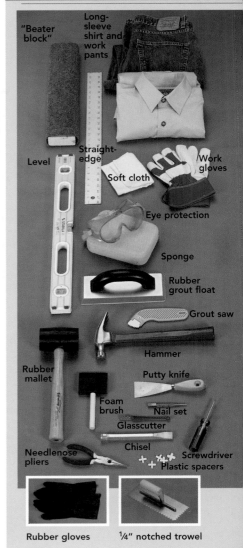

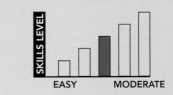

Rubber gloves    ¼" notched trowel

## SKILLS YOU NEED

- Hammering and chiseling
- Trowel work
- Grouting and sealing

## DIFFICULTY LEVEL

This project can be completed in a day or so, including drying time, depending on how many tiles need to be replaced.

# HOW TO REPLACE A CERAMIC TILE

**1** With a carbide-tipped grout saw, apply firm but gentle pressure across the grout until you expose the unglazed edges of the tile. Do not scratch the glazed tile surface. If the grout is stubborn, use a hammer and screwdriver to first tap the tile (Step 2).

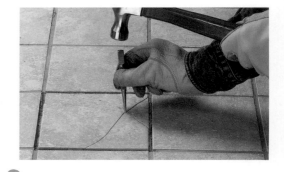

**2** If the tile is not already cracked, use a hammer to puncture the tile by tapping a nail set or center punch into it. Alternatively, if the tile is significantly cracked, use a chisel to pry up the tile.

**3** To remove the tile, insert a chisel into one of the cracks and gently tap the tile. Start at the center and chip outward so you don't damage the adjacent tiles. Be aware that cement board looks a lot like mortar when you're chiseling. Remove and discard the broken pieces.

**4** Use a putty knife to scrape away old thinset adhesive; use a chisel for poured mortar installation. Note: If the underlayment is covered with metal lathe you won't be able to get the area smooth, just clean it out the best you can. Once the adhesive is scraped from the underlayment, smooth the rough areas with sandpaper. If there are gouges in the underlayment, fill them with epoxy-based thinset mortar (for cementboard) or a floor-leveling compound (for plywood). Allow the area to completely dry.

## SAFETY FIRST

**C**hipping out a ceramic tile can create flying shards of very sharp ceramic fragments. When doing this work, use patient, gentle blows of your hammer on the chisel. Always wear eye protection when using a hammer and chisel.

## TOOL TIP

**B**efore puncturing the tile with a nail set, you may want to weaken the tile by scoring deep fracture lines into it with a glasscutter and straightedge.

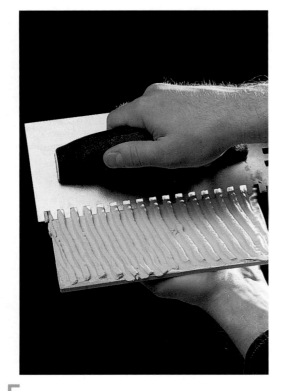

**5** Use a ¼" notched trowel to apply thinset adhesive to the back of the replacement tile. Set the tile down into the space, and use plastic spacers around the tile to make sure it is centered within the opening.

**6** Set the tile in position and press down until it is even with the adjacent tiles. Twist it a bit to get it to sit down in the mortar. Use a mallet or hammer and a block of wood covered with cloth or a carpet scrap (a "beater block") to lightly tap on the tile, setting it into the adhesive. Use a level or other straight surface to make sure the tile is level with the surrounding tiles. If necessary, continue to tap the tile until it's flush with the rest of the surrounding tiles.

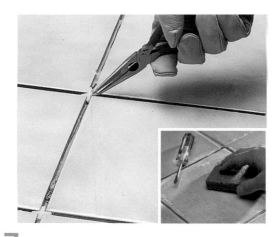

**7** Remove the spacers with needlenose pliers. Get the mortar or thinset adhesive out of the grout joints with a small screwdriver and a cloth. Also, wipe away any adhesive from the surface of the tiles, using a wet sponge. Let the area dry for 24 hours (or according to the manufacturer's recommendations).

**8** Use a putty knife to apply grout to the joints. Fill in low spots by applying and smoothing extra grout with your finger. Use the round edge of a toothbrush handle to create a concave grout line, if desired. You must now grout the joint. See page 75, Step 6.

**1** To grout and seal a large area, mix a batch of floor grout in a bucket, according to the directions on the label.

**2** Pour the grout over the tile, then use a rubber grout float or rubber squeegee to spread it over the grout joints. Press down with a wiggling motion to force the grout deeply into the joints. Then tilt the face of the float 45° and diagonally drag the float across the joints to evenly apply the grout.

**3** Let the grout set for 10 to 15 minutes, then use the grout float to remove excess grout from the surface of the tile. Hold the grout float on its edge and use a scraping motion.

### HERE'S HOW

When mixing grout for porous tile, such as quarry or natural stone, use an additive with a release agent to prevent grout from bonding to the tile surfaces.

**4** Use a barely damp sponge to wipe away excess grout from the surface of the tile. Be gentle with the joints themselves, though—you don't want to pull grout out of the joints you've just filled.

**5** Let the grout dry for about 4 hours, then polish the tile with a soft cloth.

**6** Use a foam brush to seal the grout after it cures. Do this every 1 to 2 years to protect against stains and to prevent it from crumbling.

### HERE'S HOW

To determine if your grout needs to be resealed, test the existing sealer by putting a few drops of water on a grout line. If the water beads up, the sealer is still working. If the water absorbs into the grout, it needs to be resealed.

## 15

# Replacing Parquet Tiles

Parquet is manufactured in hundreds of geometric patterns ranging from high-end, custom designs to the well-known herringbone pattern to affordable block designs. No matter what the style, all parquet floors consist of individual tiles.

PARQUET FLOORS HAVE LONG BEEN ASSOCIATED WITH ELEGANCE. LONG-LASTING and durable, parquet is still not invincible to the regular wear and tear that floors with such a reputation often endure. But don't hold back from using this type of floor to its fullest extent, because stained, burned, or damaged hardwood parquet tile is relatively easy to replace. And the following pages show you how to do just that.

# PARQUET CONSTRUCTION 101

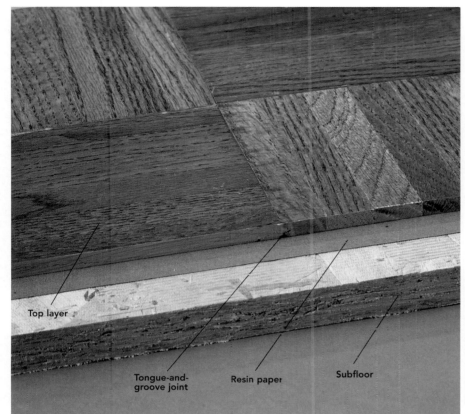

Top layer

Tongue-and-groove joint

Resin paper

Subfloor

The top layer of solid parquet is hardwood. With this type of parquet, the tiles often fit together with tongue-and-groove joints (though straight edges are also available and would be glued together and possibly nailed to the subfloor) and are adhered to resin paper, which sits on the subfloor. When replacing an individual tile, the resin paper is not replaced. Instead, the tile is adhered directly to the subfloor.

## TERMS YOU NEED TO KNOW

PLUNGE CUT—A technique used to cut out a rectangular area from the center of a piece of wood. The blade is set to cut through the exact thickness of the wood. The guide is pulled away from the saw and then the saw is turned on and eased down into the wood. Back into the line a bit and then repeat the cut for the next immediate section of wood on the cutting line.

SUBFLOOR—The base layer of wood or plywood that supports the underlayment and surface flooring.

TONGUE AND GROOVE—Carpentry joint in which the jutting edge of one board fits into the grooved end of a similar board.

# HOW TO REPLACE A PARQUET TILE

**1** For the initial plunge cut, set the depth of a circular saw to the thickness of the parquet tile. (If you don't know the thickness, see Here's How, this page.) Hold the saw so that only the top of the guide plate touches the surface of the wood; the blade, when lowered, will cut into the damaged wood block. Turn on the saw. Slowly lower the blade into the cutting line until the saw's cut guide rests flat on the floor. Make a series of four plunge cuts into the damaged tile—1" inside each edge—to make a square cutout.

**2** Use a hammer and a sharp, 1"-wide chisel to chip out the cut pieces in the center of the damaged tile. When you're removing the pieces around the edge of the cutout, make sure the beveled side of the chisel is facing the damaged area so that a clean flat edge is left along the adjacent tiles. If you need some elbow grease to remove the center pieces, use a hammer to tap a pry bar under the damaged cutout and then lean it over a scrap of 2 × 4 for leverage.

**3** Use a putty knife to scrape away the remaining adhesive on the underlayment so that the new tile will sit flush with the surrounding floor.

## HERE'S HOW

If you don't have a replacement tile, and therefore don't know how thick the tiles are, you can determine the thickness by slowly drilling through the damaged tile with a ¾" hole saw or ¾"-wide spade drill bit. Very

slowly drill through the damaged tile. Drill only a bit at a time until you bore all the way through the flooring and can see the top of the subfloor, then you can measure the depth of the board with a measuring tape. The depth will range from ⁵⁄₁₆" to ¾" thick.

Lower lip
removed

**4** Remove lower lip of groove in replacement
tile. If the replacement wood block has a tongue-
and-groove structure, remove the lower lip of the
groove so that you can press it into place. Lay the
replacement block face down onto a protective
scrap of wood and use a sharp chisel to split off
the lower lip. Lightly sand the edges.

**SAFETY FIRST**

**W**henever cutting or drilling wood, be sure
to wear protective eyewear.

**5** Apply adhesive. Use a ⅛" notched trowel to
spread a thin layer of floor adhesive onto the back
of the replacement tile and the floor. The ridges
should be about ⅛" high on the replacement tile.
The adhesive on the floor is only to make sure the
tiles are completely covered on all edges. You
want a secure bond, but you do not want adhesive
to squeeze up between the tiles.

**6** Install replacement block. Hook the tongue
of the replacement block into the groove of an
adjacent block and then use a soft mallet to gently
tap the groove side of the new block down into
place. If adhesive happens to squeeze up onto any
of the block, clean it immediately with the cleaning solvent recommended by the adhesive manufacturer. You're done!

# Replacing Floorboards

## 16

No matter how durable wood floors may be, it is guaranteed that families, friends, and neighbors will give them a run for their money. A damaged floorboard doesn't mean the entire floor is ruined. Individual wood planks or strips may be replaced.

IF YOUR HARDWOOD FLOORS HAVE A FEW DAMAGED AREAS BUT ARE OTHERWISE in good shape, you can replace the damaged floorboards. There are two ways to replace damaged floorboards: the easiest way is to create a rectangular patch, in which the immediate area of the damaged board(s) is replaced; but you can also create a more seamless, staggered pattern. Using the following instructions in this project, you can create either floor patch yourself and save some money for bigger projects down the road. Before replacing an entire board, be sure to refer to the projects on pages 14 and 28. Some damages can be fixed without replacing an entire board.

# FLOORBOARD T&G 101

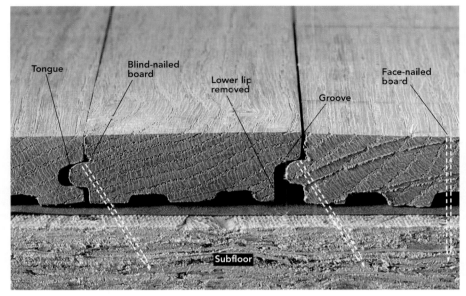

Tongue

Blind-nailed board

Lower lip removed

Groove

Face-nailed board

Subfloor

When tongue-and-groove (T&G) hardwood floors are installed, each new course is blind-nailed through the tongue before the next course is placed. The process is called "blind-nailing" because the nail is angled into the surface of the wood—you can't see it after the floor is finished because it is angled into the tongue-and-groove joint. This brings up two points: 1. You should be aware of the nails angled into the groove side of every board, so you have a better chance of avoiding them when you are cutting or drilling into floorboards. 2. The last board you put in has to be "face-nailed" (nailed through the top of the board) because you no longer have access to the tongue. The lower lip of this board is first removed, to fit into place.

**1** Draw a rectangle around the damaged area. Determine the minimal number of boards to be removed. To avoid nails, be sure to draw the line ¾" inside the outermost edge of any joints. See Here's How.

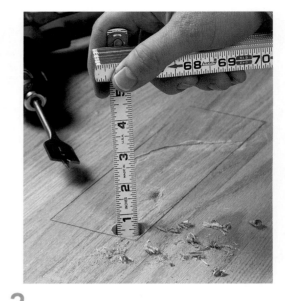

**2** Determine the depth of the boards to be cut. With a drill and ¾"-wide spade bit, slowly drill through a damaged board. Drill until you see the top of the subfloor. Measure the depth. A common depth is ⅝" or ¾". Set your circular saw to this depth.

**3** To prevent boards from chipping, place masking tape or painter's tape along the outside of the pencil lines. To create a wood cutting guide, tack a straight wood strip inside the damaged area (for easy removal, allow nails to slightly stick up). Set back the guide the distance between the saw blade and the guide edge of the circular saw.

### HERE'S HOW

It's acceptable for the two lines you've drawn lengthwise along the boards (parallel to the joints) to not line up perfectly—though it doesn't hurt if they do—because the entire board is removed. However, the lines perpendicular to the boards (the "end cuts") must be perfectly square.

**4** Align the circular saw with the wood cutting guide. Turn on the saw. Lower the blade into the cutline. Do not cut the last ¼" of the corners. Remove cutting guide. Repeat with other sides.

**5** Complete the cuts. Use a hammer and sharp chisel to completely loosen the boards from the subfloor. Make sure the chisel's beveled side is facing the damaged area for a clean edge.

**6** Remove split boards. Use a scrap 2 × 4 block for leverage and to protect the floor. With a hammer, tap a pry bar into and under the split board. Most boards pop out easily, but some may require a little pressure. Remove exposed nails with the hammer claw.

**7** Use a chisel to remove the 2 remaining strips. Again, make sure the bevel side of the chisel is facing the interior of the damaged area. Set any exposed nails with your nail set.

**8** Cut new boards. Measure the length and width of the area to be replaced. Place the new board on a sawhorse, with the section to be used hanging off the edge. Draw a pencil cutline. With saw blade on waste side of mark, firmly press the saw guide against the edge of a framing square. Measure each board separately.

**9** Use a mallet or hammer to gently tap the groove of the new board into the tongue of the existing board. To protect the tongue of the new board, use a scrap 2 × 4 or a manufacturer's block as a hammering block.

**10** Pick a drill bit with a slightly smaller diameter than an 8-penny finish nail, and drill holes at a 45° angle through the corner of the replacement piece's tongue every 3" to 4" along the new board. Hammer a 1½"-long, 8-penny finish nail through the hole into the subfloor. Use a nail set to countersink nails. Repeat until the last board.

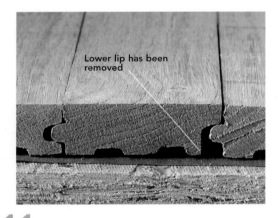

Lower lip has been removed

**11** Lay the last board face down onto a protective 2 × 4 and use a sharp chisel to split off the lower lip. This allows it to fit into place.

**12** To install the last board, hook the tongue into the groove of the old floor and then use a soft mallet to tap the groove side down into the previous board installed.

### HERE'S HOW

In older houses, existing boards may have slightly separated. In such a case, a very snug patch might draw attention to itself. To recreate the spacing gaps, place thin shims, such as metal washers, between the new board and the existing one before drilling the nail holes.

### WHAT IF . . . ?

If you accidentally dent the floor surface with a hammer, place a damp cloth on the spot and apply pressure with a hot iron. This will raise the damaged surface of the wood back to level.

**13**   Drill pilot holes angled outward: two side-by-side holes about ½" from the edges of each board, and one hole every 12" along the groove side of each board. Drive 1½"-long, 8-penny finish nails through the holes. Set nails with a nail set. Fill holes with wood putty.

**14**   Finish. Once putty is dry, sand the patch smooth with fine-grit sandpaper. Feather sand neighboring boards. Vacuum and wipe the area with a clean cloth. Apply matching wood stain or restorer; then apply 2 coats of matching finish. To find out what type of finish your floor has, see page 31.

---

**HERE'S HOW**

To make a more seamless patch, install a staggered pattern. Follow the basic instructions for the rectangular patch, with the following exceptions:

**1** Drill a series of holes into the damaged boards with a ⅝" Forstner bit or hole saw bit. Mark the drilling depth with masking tape so you do not drill into the subfloor.

**2** Split and pry out boards. Set the circular saw depth to floorboard thickness. Split damaged boards lengthwise. Cut outward from the center until the cuts intersect the holes. Chisel out wood between holes. Using a 2x4 block for leverage, pry out boards.

**3** Install new boards. Place outermost boards first, working your way in. Use a 2x4 scrap hammering block and hammer to tap the new board into place. Lay the last board on a protective 2x4 and use a sharp chisel to split off the lower lip. See Step 12 for installing last board.

As indestructible as laminate floors may seem, minor scratches caused by normal day-to-day wear and tear are unavoidable. Whether the damaged plank is close to a wall or in the middle of the floor, this project will show you how to replace it.

IN THE EVENT THAT YOU NEED TO REPLACE A LAMINATE PLANK, YOU MUST first determine how to remove the damaged plank. If you have a glueless "floating" floor it is best to unsnap and remove each plank starting at the wall and moving in until you reach the damaged plank (see page 91). However, if the damaged plank is far from the wall it is more time-efficient to cut out the damaged plank (see page 88). Fully-bonded laminate planks have adhesive all along the bottom of the plank and are secured directly to the underlayment. When you remove the damaged plank you run the risk of gouging the subfloor, so we recommend calling in a professional if you find that your laminate planks are completely glued to the subfloor.

# LAMINATE PLANKS 101

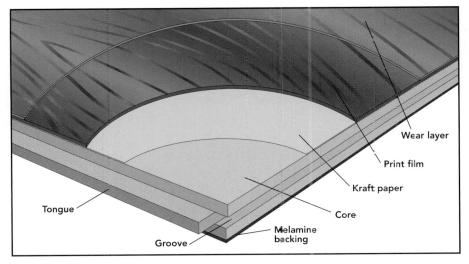

- Wear layer
- Print film
- Kraft paper
- Core
- Melamine backing
- Tongue
- Groove

From bottom to top, laminate planks are engineered to resist moisture, scratches, and dents. A melamine base layer protects the inner core layer, which is most often HDF (high-density fiberboard). This is occasionally followed by kraft paper saturated in resins for added protection and durability. The print film is a photographic layer that replicates the look of wood or ceramic. The surface is a highly protective wear layer. The tongue-and-groove planks fit together tightly and may be (according to manufacturer's instructions) glued together for added stability.

## TERMS YOU NEED TO KNOW

SUBFLOOR—The base layer of wood or plywood that supports the underlayment and surface flooring.

UNDERLAYMENT—The intermediate layer between the surface flooring material and subfloor. The rollout underlayment for laminate flooring combines a poly-water barrier and a foam cushion sound barrier.

FLOATING FLOORS—Flooring that does not fasten directly to the subfloor or underlayment, but rather "floats" on top. The flooring material is held together with a snap-together, interlocking system, either with or without adhesive at the joints. When replacing a cut out plank, you must use adhesive at the joints where the tongue-and-groove edges have been removed.

GLUELESS LAMINATE FLOORS—Flooring that does not require glue for installation, but instead relies upon a tight tongue-and-groove system.

FULLY-BONDED LAMINATE FLOORS—Laminate flooring that is attached to the subfloor with adhesive.

PLUNGE CUT—A technique used to cut out a rectangular area from the center of a piece of wood. Adjust the cut to the exact wood thickness. Turn on the saw and ease it down into the wood. Repeat along the entire cutline.

## TOOLS & SUPPLIES YOU NEED

Laminate adhesive, Cardboard scraps, Circular saw, Replacement plank, Router, Wax paper, Protective eyewear, Drill, 3/16" drill bit, Pry bar, Pliers, Damp towel, Hammer, Pencil, Marker, Wide painter's tape, Scrap of 2x4, Nail set, Suction cup, Plastic spatula, Sandpaper, Chisel

## SKILLS YOU NEED

- Hammering using a nail set
- Drilling
- Using pry bar, chisel, and pliers
- Plunge cutting with a circular saw
- Using a router

## DIFFICULTY LEVEL

SKILLS LEVEL

EASY    MODERATE

This project can be completed in less than a day, not including 24 hours for adhesive drying time.

**1** Draw a rectangle in the middle of the damaged board with a 1½" border between the rectangle and factory edges. At each rectangle corner and inside each corner of the plank, use a hammer and nail set to make indentations. At each of these indentations, drill ³⁄₁₆" holes into the plank. Only drill the depth of the plank.

**3** To remove the remaining outer edges of the damaged plank, place a scrap 2 x 4 wood block along the outside of one long cut and use it for leverage to push a pry bar under the flooring. Insert a second pry bar beneath the existing floor (directly under the joint of the adjacent plank) and use a pliers to grab the 1½" border strip in front of the pry bar. Press downward until a gap appears at the joint. Remove the border piece. Remove the opposite strip and then the two short end pieces in the same manner.

**2** To protect the floor from chipping, place painter's tape along the cutlines. Now, set the circular saw depth to the thickness of the replacement plank. (If you don't have a replacement plank, see page 82, Step 2 to determine the plank thickness.) To plunge cut the damaged plank, turn on the saw and slowly lower the blade into the cutline until the cut guide rests flat on the floor. Push the saw from the center of the line out to each end. Stop ¼" in from each corner. Use a hammer to tap a pry bar or chisel into the cutlines. Lift and remove the middle section. Place a sharp chisel between the two drill holes in each corner and strike with a hammer to complete each corner cut. Vacuum.

**4** Place a scrap of cardboard in the opening to protect the underlayment foam while you remove all of the old glue from the factory edges with a chisel. Vacuum up the wood and glue flakes.

**5** To remove the tongues on one long and one short end, lay the replacement plank face down onto a protective scrap of plywood (or 2 × 4). Clamp a straight cutting guide to the replacement plank so the distance from the guide causes the bit to align with the tongue and trim it off. Pressing the router against the cutting guide, slowly move along the entire edge of the replacement plank to remove the tongue. Clean the edges with sandpaper.

**6** Dry-fit the grooves on the replacement board into the tongues of the surrounding boards and press into place. If the board fits snugly in between the surrounding boards, pry the plank up with a manufacturer suction cup. If the plank does not sit flush with the rest of the floor, check to make sure you routered the edges off evenly. Sand any rough edges that should have been completely removed and try to fit the plank again.

**7** Set the replacement plank by applying laminate glue to the removed edges of the replacement plank and into the grooves of the existing planks. Firmly press the plank into place.

**8** Clean up glue with a damp towel. Place a strip of wax paper over the new plank and evenly distribute some books on the wax paper. Allow the adhesive to dry for 12 to 24 hours.

Filler Sticks

Color fill

Plastic putty knife

Touch-up markers

Sandpaper

Patch shallow scratches or chips with acrylic filler, latex repair putty, a filler stick or pencil, or a touch-up marker (supplied by the manufacturer to match the tint of your floor). Apply the repair putty and acrylic filler with a plastic putty knife. If the scratch is rough or there are splinters, first sand it smooth with fine sandpaper.

To fix deep gouges using a warm manufacturer's recommended burn-in knife, hold the knife against a burn-in stick of the appropriate color to match your floor. Allow the stick to melt and drip onto the damaged area until the gouge is slightly overfilled. Smooth the patch with flat strokes, using the burn-in knife. Once dry, clean the surface and correct missing grain lines with a manufacturer pen. Restore the surface finish. Note: Protect the finish immediately around the gouge by applying burn-in balm to the floor.

To fix gaps in joints, squeeze liquid filler into the gap. Using a slightly damp cloth, smooth the liquid flush with the surrounding floor. Use the manufacturer's recommended products and instructions.

TIP: Manufacturer repair kits often include all the recommended products for a specific repair. For example, most repair kits for gouges include wax to protect your surrounding floor while you are working (like burn-in balm), burn-in sticks, dewaxer and a wool pad to remove burn-in balm, fine sandpaper to smooth the patch, and a wood grain pen. The electric knife is sold separately.

If your damaged plank is close to the wall and the laminate floor is glueless, follow these steps:

**1** To remove shoe molding, wedge a chisel between the shoe molding and baseboards to create a gap and maintain that gap with wood shims. Continue this process every 6" along the wall. Locate the nails that are holding the shoe to the baseboard and use a pry bar at those locations to gently pull the shoe away from the baseboard (inset).

**2** To remove the first plank closest to the wall, use a pry bar to lift it just enough to get your hands under it and then slowly lift up and away from the adjacent plank. Continue to remove the planks that are between the shoe molding and the damaged plank with your hands. Finally, remove the damaged plank.

**3** Snap in a new replacement plank and then continue to replace the rest of the boards until you reach the wall in the same manner.

**4** Lay the shoe molding back in place along the wall. Using a nail set and hammer, countersink finish nails into the top of the shoe molding every 6 to 12" along the wall. Fill the holes with wood putty.

## 18

# Patching Major Carpet Damage

Large spills often soak into carpet quickly and then start to spread. This can permanently damage a significant portion of your carpet. In such a case, a large carpet patch is in order.

IF A RELATIVELY LARGE AREA OF CARPET IS STAINED, BURNED, WORN, OR damaged, you can replace the damaged section with a matching carpet remnant. A large patch will likely be noticeable if the surrounding carpet is worn or faded, but a clean patch will prevent further damage—no matter how much you clean it, a large stain will attract oils and debris because the surface will be different from that of the surrounding carpet.

If you don't have a leftover remnant, you still have some options: If the carpet isn't too old, you may be able to find a matching remnant at a carpet dealer. If not, consider cutting a piece from the back of a closet or from under a couch that you don't intend to move. If these options are unsatisfactory, consider using a different type of carpet altogether and extending the patch to the nearest transition, such as a door threshold or wall. This will make your carpet design unique, and no one will track your inspiration to a damaged piece of carpet!

# CARPET PATCHING 101

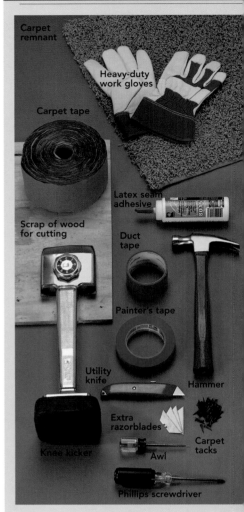

Carpet remnant

Heavy-duty work gloves

Carpet tape

Latex seam adhesive

Scrap of wood for cutting

Duct tape

Painter's tape

Utility knife

Hammer

Extra razorblades

Knee kicker

Awl

Carpet tacks

Phillips screwdriver

Before you start, be aware that even the best patching job may be noticeable if your carpet is faded or very worn. Any difference between the patch and the surrounding carpet will fade somewhat over time and become less noticeable. The difference is somewhat minimalized if you make sure the carpet nap of the patch matches the surrounding area (inset).

## SKILLS YOU NEED

- Using simple knee kicker
- Cutting
- Hammering tacks
- Gluing

## TERMS YOU NEED TO KNOW

WALL-TO-WALL CARPET—Two layers of woven backing are laid over separate padding. Installed by stretching onto tackless strips.

CUSHION-BACKED CARPET—One layer of woven backing is manufactured with a foam backing bonded to its underside and needs no additional padding. It is glued to the floor, rather than being installed under tension. Cushion-backed carpet was more common 15 years ago than it is now.

KNEE KICKER—A tool used for stretching carpet. The teeth at the front end of the tool grip the carpet; the back end is shaped so the user can apply forward pressure with the knee.

## DIFFICULTY LEVEL

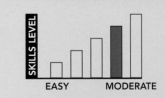

SKILLS LEVEL

EASY          MODERATE

This project can be completed in a couple of hours, not including adhesive drying time.

**1** Use a utility knife to cut four strips from a carpet remnant, each a little wider and longer than the cuts you plan to make around the damaged part of your carpet. Most wall-to-wall carpet is installed under tension; so to relieve that tension, set the knee kicker 6" to 1 ft. from the area to be cut out and nudge it forward (toward the patch area). If you create a hump in the carpet, you've pushed too hard and need to back off. Now place one of the strips upside down in front of the knee kicker and tack it to the floor at 2" to 4" intervals. Repeat the same process on the other three sides.

**2** Use a marker to draw arrows on tape. Fan the carpet with your hand to see which direction the fibers are woven, and then use the pieces of tape to mark that direction on both the carpet surrounding the damaged area and the remnant you intend to use as a patch. Place a carpet remnant on plywood and cut out a carpet patch slightly larger than the damaged section, using a utility knife. As you cut, use a Phillips screwdriver to push carpet tufts or loops away from the cutting line. Trim loose pile, and then place the patch right side up over the damaged area.

---

### TOOL TIP

**K**nee kickers have teeth that grab the carpet backing. These teeth should be set to grab the backing without grabbing the padding. There is an adjustable knob to do this. You can tell if the knee kicker is grabbing the padding by the increased pressure needed to move it forward. To release the tension just before a damaged area of carpet you intend to patch, place the feet on the floor and use your knee to press it toward the damaged area.

**3** Tack one edge of the patch through the damaged carpet and into the floor, making sure the patch covers the entire damaged area. Use a utility knife to cut out the damaged carpet, following the border of the new patch as a template. If you cut into the carpet padding, use duct tape to mend it. Remove the patch and the damaged carpet square.

**5** Line up your arrows and press the patch into place. Take care not to press too much, because glue that squeezes up onto the newly laid carpet creates a mess. Use an awl to free tufts or loops of pile crushed in the seam. Lightly brush the pile of the patch to make it blend with the surrounding carpet. Leave the patch undisturbed for 24 hours. Check the drying time on the adhesive used and wait at least this long before removing the carpet tacks.

**4** Cut four lengths of carpet seam tape, each about 1" longer than an edge of the cut out area, using a utility knife or scissors. Cover half of each strip with a thin layer of seam adhesive and then slip the coated edge of each strip, sticky side up, along the underside edges of the original carpet. Apply more adhesive to the exposed half of tape, and use enough adhesive to fill in the tape weave.

---

### WHAT IF . . . ?

If you have cushion-backed, fully-bonded carpet, you can follow the instructions above to make a large patch, except:

1. You won't need a knee kicker.

2. Use a putty knife to scrape away any dried cement from the hole you make.

3. Apply multi-purpose flooring adhesive to the floor with a $^3/_{32}$" trowel.

4. Instead of seam tape, just use a thin bead of cushion-back seam adhesive along the perimeter of the hole.

# Painting Wood Floors

## 19

Just when it appears as though you've hit a wall in reviving your tired, wornout wood floor, try a coat of paint to bring back its brilliance. You'll be pleasantly surprised with the paint's ability to not only disguise flaws but its ability to add warmth and character to the room.

PAINT IS A QUICK, COST-EFFECTIVE WAY TO COVER UP WOOD FLOORS THAT may need work, but a floor doesn't have to be distressed or damaged to benefit from painting. Floors in perfect condition in both formal and informal spaces can be decorated with paint to add color and personality. For example, one could unify a space by extending a painted floor through a hallway to a staircase. And stencil designs or faux finishes can make an oversized room feel cozy and inviting. There are even techniques for disguising worn spots. One such disguising method also happens to create a fun, yet classical design: the checkerboard pattern allows homeowners to hide worn boards under a darker color while still maintaining a unique floor. Due to its versatility, we include instructions for a checkerboard pattern at the end of this project.

# FLOOR PAINTING 101

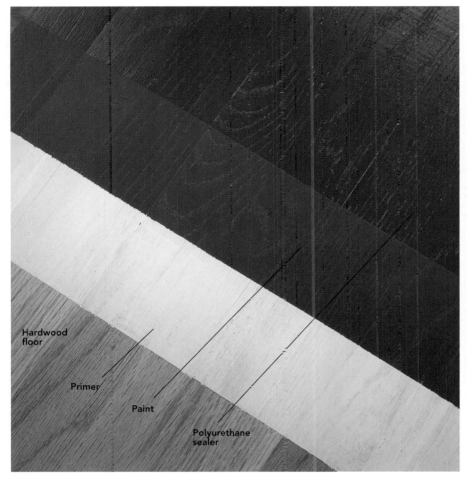

Hardwood floor

Primer

Paint

Polyurethane sealer

To paint a wood floor you must apply primer first; then you apply the paint and you follow that with a polyurethane sealer. Make sure the products you choose are specifically for floors.

## TERMS YOU NEED TO KNOW

LACQUER THINNER—A strong, highly flammable solvent such as ethyl alcohol, ethyl acetate and toluene that is used to dilute, dissolve and clean up lacquer based paints, ink and adhesive residue.

PRIMER—A specially-formulated paint that is used to seal raw surfaces and to provide a base coat of paint that succeeding finish coats can better adhere to.

WATER-BASED POLYURETHANE—A clear finish used for coating natural or stained wood that provides a durable, glossy surface that is highly resistant to water, is just as durable as oil-based polyurethane, is easier to clean-up, and does not produce a yellowing discoloration.

SEALER—A finish coating, either clear or pigmented, that is applied on top of the paint.

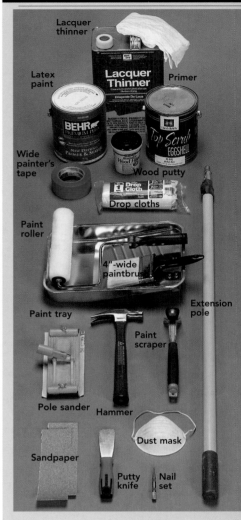

Lacquer thinner

Latex paint

Primer

Wide painter's tape

Wood putty

Drop cloths

Paint roller

4"-wide paintbrush

Paint tray

Extension pole

Paint scraper

Pole sander

Hammer

Dust mask

Sandpaper

Putty knife

Nail set

## SKILLS YOU NEED

• Cleaning and sanding
• Using a hammer and nail set
• Using a paintbrush and roller

## DIFFICULTY LEVEL

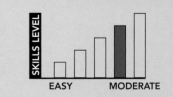

SKILLS LEVEL

EASY    MODERATE

This project can be completed in a day (not including drying time), depending upon how much prep work is needed and how large the room is.

**1** Prepare the painting area by first moving furniture. Lift pieces instead of dragging them to prevent gouges. Sweep or vacuum.

**2** Use a paint scraper to remove smooth rough spots. Use a pole sander to sand with the grain of the wood. For coarse wood, use medium-grit sandpaper. Scuff glossy hardwoods with fine sandpaper (#120) for good adhesion.

**3** When finished sanding, sweep or vacuum. Use a damp cloth to remove fine dust. Use a cloth dampened with lacquer thinner for a final cleaning. If you see any nail sticking up, tap them down with a hammer and nail set.

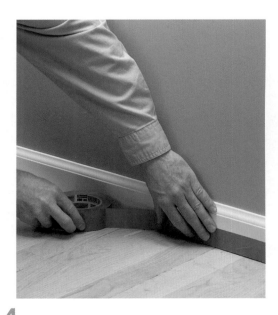

**4** Protect the baseboards with wide painter's tape. Press the tape edges down so paint doesn't seep underneath.

**5** Mix primer well (see Step 6 for mixing technique). Use a 4"-wide brush to apply the primer around the perimeter of the room. Then paint the remaining floor with a roller on an extension pole. Allow the primer to dry.

**6** To mix paint, pour half of the paint into another can, stirring the paint in both containers with a wooden stir stick before recombining them. As you stir, you want a smooth consistency.

**7** Paint. Use a 4" brush to apply a semi-gloss paint around the border. To paint the rest of the floor, use a roller on an extension pole. Always roll from a dry area to a wet area to minimize lap lines. Allow paint to dry. Apply second coat of paint. Allow to dry.

**8** Apply 2 or 3 coats of a matte-finish, water-based polyurethane sealer, using a painting pad on a pole. Allow the paint to dry. Sand with a pole sander, using fine sandpaper. Clean up dust with a tack cloth.

If your wood floor is in poor condition, it can be camouflaged with a design, such as a classic checkerboard pattern. Proper preparation is essential for lasting results. If you've already painted the floor based on the instructions from the first half of this project, you are well on your way and you have the base color already painted. You just have to paint in the darker colored squares (skip to Step 3).

**1** Remove the finish of a previously stained and sealed wood floor by sanding the surface with sandpaper on a pole, using fine-grit sandpaper. Alternatively, you may use a power sander with fine-grit sandpaper. Vacuum the entire floor, then wipe it with a tack cloth to remove all sanding dust.

**2** Use painter's tape to cover the baseboards. Paint the entire floor with the lighter of the two paint colors. Allow the paint to dry thoroughly.

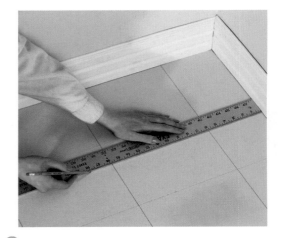

**3** Measure the entire floor. Now, determine the size of squares you'll use. Plan the design so the areas of the floor with the highest visibility, such as the main entrance, have full squares. Place partial squares along the walls in less conspicuous areas. Mark the design lines on the floor, using a straightedge and pencil.

**4** Using painter's tape, outline the squares that are to remain light in color. Press firmly along all edges of the tape, using a putty knife, to create a tight seal.

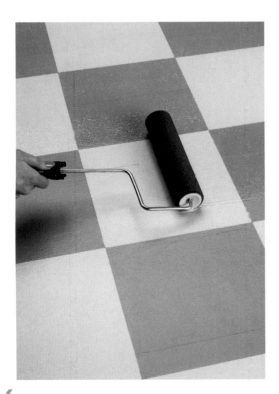

**6** After all of the paint has completely dried, apply a coat of high-gloss clear finish, using a paint roller or paint pad with a pole extension. Allow the finish to dry.

**5** Paint the remaining squares with the dark paint color. Paint in small areas at a time. Once you have painted the entire box and a few surrounding boxes, remove the masking tape from the painted squares. Be sure to remove the tape before the paint completely dries.

### HERE'S HOW

For an even longer lasting painted floor, allow the finish to dry and then sand the floor with fine-grit sandpaper. Use an extension pole with sandpaper to sand the entire floor with ease. Apply two coats of satin clear finish.

### SAFETY FIRST

When sanding, wear a dust mask, safety glasses, and work gloves. When painting, use a respirator and make sure the area is well ventilated.

## 20

# Removing Resilient Flooring

If adhesives are not properly removed before installing new resilient floor-ing, the oils may chemically react to the new material and produce a yel-low discoloration, essentially destroying the vinyl floor. These spots cannot be removed with cleaning products. In these cases, the old resilient floor-ing should be removed entirely before you install new flooring.

REMOVING GLUED-DOWN RESILIENT FLOORING IS LABOR INTENSIVE, BUT IT'S necessary to do so if the surface is in very poor condition (or if you plan to replace the old resilient flooring with ceramic tile). Oils that cause yellow discoloration can eventually dry out and crack or seep through the vinyl, damaging new floor laid on top of it. Moreover, any unevenness or debris under the old vinyl will clearly show through new resilient flooring.

Note: It is true that resilient floor can serve as the foundation for most new floorings, includ-ing resilient flooring, hardwood, or carpet, but only if the existing surface is smooth and sound. Even if the existing flooring has loose seams, small tears, or air bubbles, then you must apply embossing leveler to the entire floor and let it dry before laying new resilient flooring. Alternatively, you can lay a new ¼" plywood underlayment over the old floor or you can remove the entire subfloor with the vinyl flooring and lay a new subfloor. These meth-ods are worth consideration if you find that the subfloor is being heavily damaged as you begin to remove full-spread sheet vinyl, but they are also very time-consuming and require a considerable amount of precision.

# SHEET INSTALLATION 101

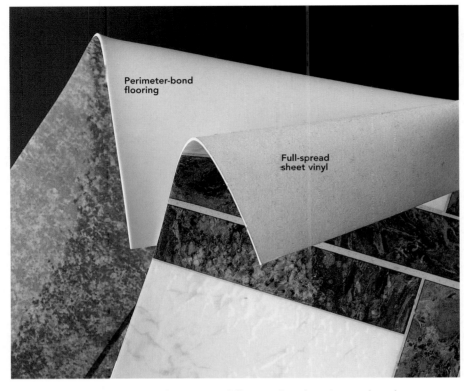

Perimeter-bond flooring

Full-spread sheet vinyl

Resilient sheet vinyl comes in full-spread and perimeter-bond styles. Full-spread sheet vinyl has felt-paper backing and is secured with adhesive that's spread over the entire floor before installation. Perimeter-bond flooring, identifiable by its smooth, white PVC backing, is laid directly on the underlayment and is secured by adhesive spread along the edges and seams.

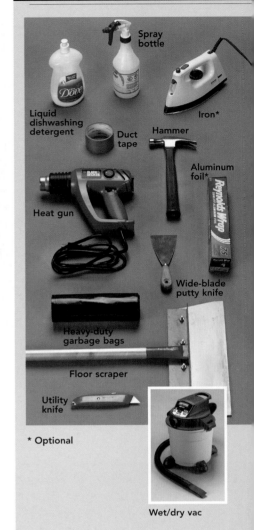

## TOOLS & SUPPLIES YOU NEED

Spray bottle

Liquid dishwashing detergent

Iron*

Duct tape

Hammer

Heat gun

Aluminum foil*

Wide-blade putty knife

Heavy-duty garbage bags

Floor scraper

Utility knife

* Optional

Wet/dry vac

## TERMS YOU NEED TO KNOW

SUBFLOOR—The base layer of wood or plywood that supports the underlayment and surface flooring.

UNDERLAYMENT—The intermediate layer between the surface flooring material and the subfloor.

PERIMETER-BOND SHEET VINYL—A synthetic resilient flooring that is installed in a single sheet, cut to fit the room it will be installed in, and glued to the underlayment at the room's edges.

FULL-SPREAD SHEET VINYL—A synthetic resilient flooring that is installed in a single sheet, cut to fit the room it will be installed in, and glued to the underlayment on a full-room bed of adhesive.

FLOOR SCRAPER—Designed like a shovel, a floor scraper removes resilient flooring products and scrapes off leftover adhesives or backings. The long handle provides leverage and force, and it allows you to work in a comfortable standing position.

## SKILLS YOU NEED

- Cutting with a utility knife
- Scraping
- Using a heat gun

## DIFFICULTY LEVEL

SKILLS LEVEL

EASY          MODERATE

This project can be completed in a few hours.

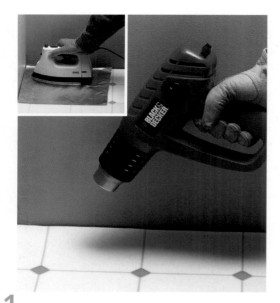

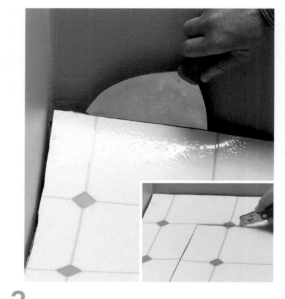

**1** Remove baseboards (see page 123, Step 4). Beginning in a corner of the room, slowly move a heat gun back and forth 4 to 6" above the floor until you can pry up the corner. Alternatively, to use an iron, place aluminum foil on the floor to prevent melting or burning the floor, and keep the temperature at a low setting (inset).

**2** Once the adhesive is warm, insert a wide-blade putty knife under the loosened corner and pry back the flooring. If the glue is only around the perimeter of the room, measure from the wall to the approximate point where the glue stops and cut a strip that wide along the entire perimeter of the room (inset). Go on to Step 3, knowing you will remove the strip you just cut along the wall last.

**3** With a utility knife, cut the flooring into strips about three feet wide (or smaller, if you find smaller strips are easier to handle and have the extra time needed for extra cutting and rolling). If you have perimeter-installed sheet flooring, start cutting the strips inside the perimeter cut you made in Step 2. Simply roll up the strips and bind them with duck tape (inset).

**4** Start pulling up the strips by hand. Grip the material close to the floor to minimize tearing. Dispose of the waste in heavy-duty construction garbage bags.

**5** Scrape the remaining sheet vinyl and backing, using a floor scraper. Use a hammer to tap a putty knife under loose edges to chip apart pieces.

**6** For stubborn spots, peel up as much of the floor covering as possible, using a putty knife. Spray a solution of water and liquid dishwashing detergent under the surface layer to separate the backing. With the help of the detergent, continue to use the putty knife to scrape up the stubborn patches.

**7** For very sticky and stubborn glue, hold a heat gun about 4 to 6" above the floor. Constantly move the heat gun as you scrape the gooey mess into a pile with a wide-blade putty knife. Occasionally pick up the pile of glue and dispose of it, and wipe the putty knife clean.

**8** Now you just need to sweep up the debris and clean up with a wet/dry vacuum. To contain the dust, fill the wet vac with about 1" of water.

### HERE'S HOW

Some old linoleum is secured to the floor with a tar-based adhesive. Tar-based adhesives are dark or tan colored and can be scrubbed away with steel wool and mineral spirits (or paint thinner).

# Removing Carpet

## 21

When removing fully-bonded, cushion-backed carpet, be prepared to find carpet adhesive and foam padding on the floor underneath. It is a time-consuming process to remove the adhesive, but your new floor is well worth the effort needed to properly prepare a clean, level underlayment.

REMOVING CARPET IS NECESSARY IF IT HAS BEEN BADLY DAMAGED OR YOU ARE ready to install a different type of flooring. It is time-consuming work, but you can save money by removing carpet even if you intend to hire someone to install new flooring. Carpet is either installed with tack strips along the perimeter of a room, with adhesive spread along the perimeter of the room, or with adhesive spread along the entire floor. We address how each type of carpet should be removed in the following pages.

# CARPET BACKING 101

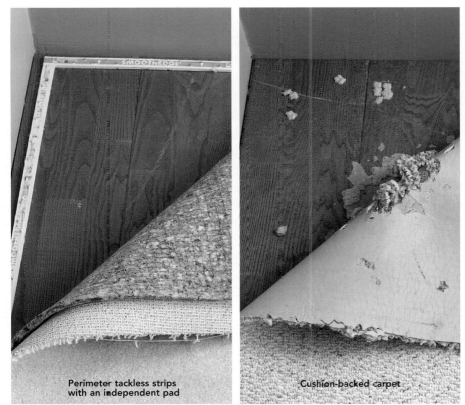

Perimeter tackless strips with an independent pad

Cushion-backed carpet

Wall-to-wall carpet is stretched and secured to tackless strips along the perimeter of the room. Once lifted from the strips, the carpet and pad can be rolled up. The tackless strips are often nailed down and must be removed. Cushion-backed carpet has a foam backing bonded to it. It is secured to the floor with general-purpose adhesive. When removing this carpet, pieces of the pad will stick to the floor. Removing all of the stubborn pieces requires time and a considerable amount of effort.

## TERMS YOU NEED TO KNOW

SUBFLOOR—The base layer of wood or plywood that supports the underlayment and surface flooring.

WALL-TO-WALL CARPET—Carpet with two layers of woven backing. Usually, it's laid over separate padding. Installed by stretching onto tackless strips.

CUSHION-BACKED CARPET—One layer of woven backing is manufactured with a foam backing bonded to its underside and needs no additional padding. Usually, it's glued to the floor, rather than being installed under tension.

TACKLESS STRIPS ("TACK STRIPS")—Plywood strips with 2 to 3 rows of sharp nails angled away from the center of the room. The strips are installed along the perimeter to hold wall-to-wall carpet in place.

## TOOLS & SUPPLIES YOU NEED

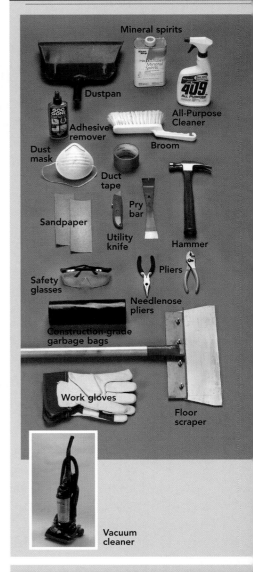

Mineral spirits
Dustpan
Adhesive remover
All-Purpose Cleaner
Dust mask
Broom
Duct tape
Pry bar
Sandpaper
Utility knife
Hammer
Safety glasses
Pliers
Needlenose pliers
Construction-grade garbage bags
Work gloves
Floor scraper

Vacuum cleaner

## SKILLS YOU NEED

- Cutting
- Using a pry bar
- Pulling up staples

## DIFFICULTY LEVEL

SKILLS LEVEL

EASY          MODERATE

This project can be completed in a day.

# HOW TO REMOVE CARPET

**1** Because you're about to be handling your old carpet for a few hours, vacuum the entire floor thoroughly.

**3** Use pliers to grab the carpet fibers along the edge of the room; then lift the carpet to release it from the tack strips. Continue to release the carpet from the tack strip along the entire perimeter of the room.

**2** Use a utility knife to cut around metal threshold strips. Use a flat pry bar to lift up the strips until they release from the floor. Dispose the strips in construction-grade garbage bags. You may be able to pull the carpet up without removing the baseboards—try Step 3—but if you find the baseboards are in the way, see page 123, Step 4, for instructions on how to remove them.

### WHAT IF . . . ?

If you do not find tackless strips, your carpet is secured with adhesive—either around the perimeter or everywhere. If it's just around the perimeter, pull back the carpet in a corner of the room until it is no longer bonded to the floor with adhesive. From that point, measure out away from the wall about 1 ft. past the glue and cut around the perimeter of the room, using a utility knife. For now, leave one wall side uncut. This side will hold the carpet in place when you begin to cut strips in Step 4. If the glue is everywhere, skip to page 111.

**4** Use your utility knife to cut the carpet into strips. Once part of the first strip of carpet is lifted, lay a scrap 2 × 4 under the carpet and use that as a cutting base—this step is necessary only if you want to protect the floor underneath (for example, if you have wood floors). After the first strip is cut, set the board on top of the carpet and fold the carpet back over the board, cutting from the underside. You may be able to cut the carpet pad and carpet at the same time; if not, you can cut the carpet pad separately later. Cut the strips into sizes that are manageable to you.

**5** Roll up the strips of carpet and secure them with duct tape. You may have to pull up on the strips with some effort if the carpet pad is stapled down. If you were not able to cut through the carpet pad, you will have to cut that into strips and roll the strips up once the carpet is removed. If you have perimeter-bonded carpet you must now remove the remaining perimeter piece glued to the floor (see page 111 for tips on loosening adhesive).

**6** Sweep up disintegrated pieces of carpet padding and put it into a construction-grade garbage bag. If the pad was held down with staples, don't clean away the bits of pad still attached to the staples—the padding makes it easier to find and remove the staples.

**TOOL TIP**

Carpet is easier to cut from the backside, so after you make an initial cut, roll it back onto itself and cut from underneath. You may also find it easier to cut if you roll the carpet over a 2x4 board, using the board as a cutting board. If you ever have to cut through the carpet from the top, be sure to lift the carpet well off the floor before cutting to avoid damaging the floor underneath.

**7** To remove tack strips, slowly and patiently lift the strips up with a pry bar. Place a thin piece of hard material (like a piece of ⅛" wood veneer) under the pry bar to protect the floor. Tack strips are attached to the floor with small nails spaced approximately 6 to 8" apart. The pry bar is most effective when placed directly under these points. If it is difficult to insert the pry bar under the tack strip in places, use a hammer to tap the short bent end of the pry bar underneath the tack strip where it is attached by a nail; then pry back.

**8** Using pliers, remove all of the remaining staples. Instead of pulling straight up, grab and twist the staples loose. Then pull them up.

**HERE'S HOW**

If you want to use the long part of the pry bar instead of the short bent end, make sure you cover the bent end with your gloved hand so that you don't accidentally scrape the floor while you're prying up with the other end.

**WHAT IF . . . ?**

If a staple is too close to the surface to get a grip on it, use a pair of side cutters to cut through the middle of the staple. Use a utility knife to separately lift up the two sections. Finally, grab the two sides, one at a time, with a pliers. This is tedious, difficult work, so if you can avoid cutting staples, do so.

Carpet installed with adhesive requires a few different steps, as follows.

**1** To remove cushion-backed carpet or carpet pads glued to the floor, use a utility knife to cut strips and pull up as much of the carpet as you can.

**2** Apply the minimum amount of mineral spirits necessary to soften the remaining adhesive and carpet padding; then use a flooring scraper to remove the adhesive. Choose a scraper that will not scratch or gouge the floors.

To remove yellow adhesive, saturate the area with an all-purpose adhesive remover. Allow the remover to sit on the adhesive for 5 minutes (or according to the manufacturer's recommendations), and then use a putty knife to scrape up the remaining adhesive.

To remove tar-based adhesive, which is dark or tan colored, saturate a cloth with mineral spirits and blot the adhesive until it softens. If the adhesive doesn't release with the cloth, use a putty knife to scrape it up.

# Sealing Concrete Floors

## 22

Although concrete is most common in garages and basements, it is not limited to these parts of the house. Along with stainless steel appliances, warehouse and loft construction, and industrial design, concrete floors are part of today's design trends, making concrete maintenance and repair increasingly relevant to today's homeowner.

CONCRETE IS A VERSATILE BUILDING MATERIAL. MOST PEOPLE ARE ACCUSTOMED to thinking of concrete primarily as a utilitarian substance, but it can also mimic a variety of flooring types and be a colorful and beautiful addition to any room.

Whether your concrete floor is a practical surface for the garage or an artistic statement of personal style in your dining room, it should be sealed. Concrete is a hard and durable building material, but it is also porous. Consequently, concrete floors are susceptible to staining. Many stains can be removed with the proper cleaner, but sealing and painting prevents oil, grease, and other stains from penetrating the surface in the first place; thus, cleanup is a whole lot easier.

# CONCRETE SEALING 101

Even after degreasing a concrete floor, residual grease or oils can create serious adhesion problems for coatings of sealant or paint. To check to see whether your floor has been adequately cleaned, pour a glass of water on the concrete floor. If it is ready for sealing, the water will soak into the surface quickly and evenly. If the water beads, you may have to clean it again. Detergent used in combination with a steam cleaner can remove stubborn stains better than a cleaner alone.

There are four important reasons to seal your concrete floor:

- To protect the floor from dirt, oil, grease, chemicals, and stains
- To dust-proof the surface
- To protect the floor from abrasion and sunlight exposure
- To repel water and protect the floor from freeze-thaw damage

## TERMS YOU NEED TO KNOW

CONCRETE—A mixture of portland cement, water, and mineral aggregate (usually sand and gravel). Sometimes fly ash, pozzolans, or other additives are included in the mix.

ACID ETCHING—This is a technique in which acid is used to open the pores in concrete surfaces so a sealer can bond to it.

## TOOLS & SUPPLIES YOU NEED

## SKILLS YOU NEED

- Cleaning
- Sweeping
- Painting floors
- Vacuuming
- Working with strong acids

## DIFFICULTY LEVEL

This project can be completed in a weekend.

**1** Clean and prepare the surface by first sweeping up all debris. Next, remove all surface muck: mud, wax, and grease. Finally, remove existing paints or coatings. See the chapter on cleaning concrete for tips on what to use to remove a variety of common stains (page 17).

**2** Saturate the surface with clean water. The surface needs to be wet before acid etching. Use this opportunity to check for any areas where water beads up. If water beads on the surface, contaminants still need to be cleaned off with a suitable cleaner or chemical stripper.

## HERE'S HOW

Prepare the concrete for sealer application by acid etching. Etching opens the pores in concrete surfaces, allowing sealers to bond with it. All smooth or dense concrete surfaces, such as garage floors, should be etched before applying stain. The surface should feel gritty, like 120-grit sandpaper, and allow water to penetrate it. If you're not sure whether your floor needs to be etched or not, it's better to etch. If you don't etch when it is needed, you have to remove the sealer residue before trying again. This easily becomes a timely process that is best to avoid from the get-go.

THERE IS A VARIETY OF ACID ETCHING PRODUCTS AVAILABLE:

CITRIC ACID is a biodegradable acid that does not produce chlorine fumes. It is the safest etcher and the easiest to use, but it may not be strong enough for some very smooth concretes.

SULFAMIC ACID is less aggressive than phosphoric acid or muriatic acid, and it is perhaps the best compromise between strength of solution and safety.

PHOSPHORIC ACID is a stronger and more noxious acid than the previous two, but it is considerably less dangerous than muriatic acid. It is currently the most popular etching choice.

MURIATIC ACID (Hydrochloric Acid) is an extremely dangerous acid that quickly reacts and creates very strong fumes. This is an etching solution of last resort. It should only be used by professionals or by the most serious DIYers.

NOTE: **Never add water to acid—only add acid to water.**

**3** Test your acid-tolerant pump sprayer with water to make sure it releases a wide, even mist. Once you have the spray nozzle set, check the manufacturer's instructions for the etching solution and fill the pump sprayer with the recommended amount of water.

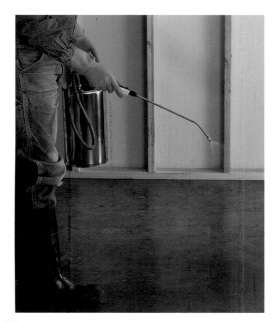

**5** Apply the acid solution. Using the sprinkling can or acid-tolerant pump spray unit, evenly apply the diluted acid solution over the concrete floor. Do not allow acid solution to dry at any time during the etching and cleaning process. Etch small areas at a time, 10 × 10 ft. or smaller. If there is a slope, begin on the low side of the slope and work upward.

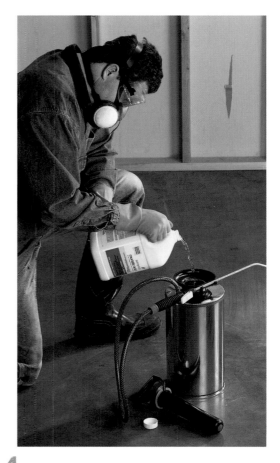

**4** Add the acid etching contents to the water in the acid-tolerant pump sprayer (or sprinkling can). Follow the directions (and mixing proportions) specified by the manufacturer. Use caution.

### SAFETY FIRST

All of these acids are dangerous. Use caution.

With any of these acid etches it is critical that there be adequate ventilation and that you wear protective clothing including:

- Safety goggles
- Respirator
- Rubber gloves
- Rubber boots
- Long pants and a long-sleeve shirt (to prevent acid contact with the skin)

**6** Use a stiff bristle broom or scrubber to work the acid solution into the concrete. Let the acid sit for 5–10 minutes, or as indicated by the manufacturer's directions. A mild foaming action indicates that the product is working. If no bubbling or fizzing occurs, it means there is still grease, oil, or a concrete treatment on the surface that is interfering with the etching product.

**7** Once the fizzing has stopped, the acid has finished reacting with the alkaline concrete surface and formed pH-neutral salts. Neutralize any remaining acid with an alkaline-base solution. Put a gallon of water in a 5-gallon bucket and then stir in an alkaline-base neutralizer. Using a stiff bristle broom, make sure the concrete surface is completely covered with the solution. Continue to sweep until the fizzing stops.

## WHAT IF . . . ?

If no fizzing occurs when the acid solution is put on the concrete, stop the process and clean the surface. Use a nylon bristle scrub brush to scrub the area with hot liquid dish soap and water, laundry soap and water, or a biodegradable degreasing cleaner. You can also try using a pressure washer. For specific stains, see the chapter on cleaning concrete (page 16). If degreasing doesn't solve the problem, the concrete may already be sealed with a concrete sealer. A surface sealer can only be removed mechanically by abrasive blasting; penetrant sealers may not be removable at all.

**8** Use a garden hose with a pressure nozzle or, ideally, a pressure washer in conjunction with a stiff bristle broom to thoroughly rinse the concrete surface. Rinse the surface 2 to 3 times. Reapply the acid (repeat Steps 5, 6, 7, and 8).

**9** If you have any leftover acid you can make it safe for your septic system by mixing more alkaline solution in the 5-gallon bucket and carefully pouring the acid from the spray unit into the bucket until all of the fizzing stops.

**10** Use a wet-vacuum to clean up the mess. Some sitting acids and cleaning solutions can harm local vegetation, damage your drainage system, and are just plain environmentally unfriendly. Check your local disposal regulations for proper disposal of the neutralized spent acid.

**11** To check for residue, rub a dark cloth over a small area of concrete. If any white residue appears, continue the rinsing process. Check for residue again. You may be sick of the cleanup by now, but an inadequate acid rinse is even worse than not acid etching at all when it's time to add the sealant.

### TOOL TIP

**M**ix one of these alkaline products with a gallon of water for a suitable acid-neutralizing solution:

- One cup of ammonia
  OR
- Four cups of gardener's lime
  OR
- A generous amount of baking soda
  OR
- 4 oz. of "Simple Green" cleaning solution

**12** Let the concrete dry for at least 24 hours and sweep up dust, dirt, and particles leftover from the acid etching process. Your concrete should now have the consistency of 120-grit sandpaper and be able to accept concrete sealants.

## TOOL TIP

**THERE ARE BASICALLY TWO CATEGORIES OF SEALERS:**

**FILM FORMERS** create a barrier on the concrete's surface, blocking penetration of water and contaminants and providing a gloss or sheen. Film formers do not allow the concrete to breathe; they may trap moisture beneath the concrete surface. In cold areas this results in cracks due to the moisture freezing and expanding.

**PENETRANTS** increase water repellency and stain resistance by actually penetrating into the concrete surface to a depth of about 1 to 4 mils, providing an invisible protection without changing the surface appearance.

**13** Once etched, clean, and dry, your concrete is ready for clear sealer or liquid repellent. Mix the sealer in a bucket with a stir stick. Lay painter's tape down for a testing patch. Apply sealer to this area and allow to dry to ensure desired appearance. Concrete sealers tend to make the surface slick when wet. Add an anti-skid additive to aid with traction, especially on stairs.

## WHAT IF . . . ?

The most common sealing practice is to use clear sealant but there are also stained sealants and paints.

If you decide to paint instead of applying a clear or stained sealant, be sure to use paint designed for concrete floors. Also, once the paint has dried for a few days, apply two or three coats of water-based polyurethane.

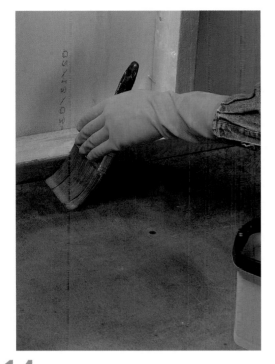

**14** Use wide painter's tape to protect walls and then, using a good quality 4"-wide synthetic bristle paintbrush, coat the perimeter with sealer.

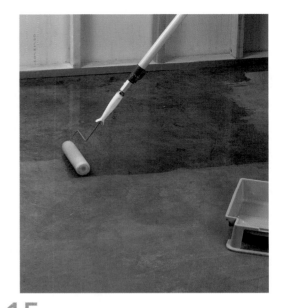

**15** Use a long-handled paint roller with at least ½" nap to apply an even coat to the rest of the surface. Do small sections at a time (about 2' × 3'). Work in one orientation (e.g., north and south). Avoid lap marks by always maintaining a wet edge. Do not work the area once the coating has partially dried; this could cause it to lift from the surface. Allow surface to dry according to the manufacturer's instructions, usually 8 to 12 hours, minimum.

**16** Apply a second coat in the opposite direction to the first coat, so if the first coat was north to south, the second coat should be east to west.

**17** Clean tools, wet/dry vac and spray equipment with clean, warm water or mineral spirits.

## 23

# Refinishing Hardwood Floors

Reviving your hardwood floors is definitely worth the hard work. By refinishing a tired-looking floor you suddenly realize why hardwood floors are so durable and long-lasting: They clean up beautifully.

MAKING WORN AND DULL HARDWOOD FLOORS LOOK NEW AGAIN DRAMATICALLY IMPROVES THE APPEARANCE OF A HOME. And the fact that very old hardwood floors can be completely restored to showroom condition is one of their real advantages over other types of flooring. Refinishing floors is time-consuming, messy, and disruptive to your household routine. Depending on the size of the room, be prepared to devote a weekend, minimally, to this project.

If you don't want to do the entire job yourself, you can still save money by doing some prep work yourself. Professionals often add on additional fees for removing and replacing shoe molding (see page 123), nailing or gluing down loose boards (pages 42 and 43), filling gouges and dents with wood putty (page 43), setting protruding nails, putting up plastic (page 122), cleaning the floor (page 14), and even moving furniture (page 98, Step 1).

NOTE: If your floors are less than $\frac{1}{2}$" thick, you should consult a floor contractor to see if the floors can withstand the refinishing process.

# REFINISHING 101

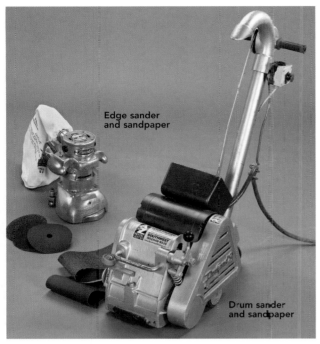

Edge sander
and sandpaper

Drum sander
and sandpaper

Refinishing a floor
requires some heavy
machinery, namely
drum and edge
sanders. These, along
with the accompany-
ing sandpaper, may
be rented from home
stores or floor rental
establishments.

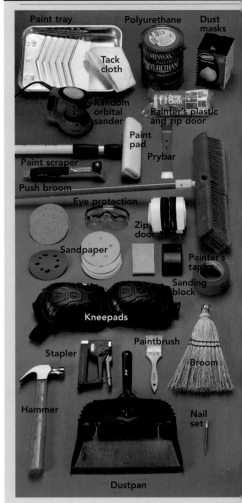

Paint tray — Polyurethane — Dust masks

Tack cloth

Random orbital sander — Painter's plastic and zip door

Paint pad

Paint scraper — Prybar

Push broom

Eye protection

Zip door

Sandpaper — Painter's tape

Sanding block

Kneepads

Paintbrush

Stapler — Broom

Hammer — Nail set

Dustpan

## TYPES OF FINISHES

**SURFACE FINISH**—A floor finish applied to the wood surface, providing a harder and more durable coating than a sealer with a wax covering (for example, polyurethane (oil- or water-based) varnish, shellac, and lacquer).

**PENETRANT FINISH**—Penetrant floor finishes seep into the wood pores and become an integral part of the wood (for example, stains or sealers).

**STAINS**—Penetrants that alter the natural color of the wood. They can be used with a surface finish or protected with a sealer and wax.

**SEALERS**—Either clear or tinted penetrants that need to be protected with a wax or surface finish.

**WAX**—Wood floors not protected with a surface finish need to be covered with a coat of liquid, non-waterbased wax. Wax is not as durable as surface finish; peri-odically, it must be reapplied. The advantage is that patched areas easily blend in.

## SKILLS YOU NEED

- Operating power sanders
- Using a large stapler
- Scraping floor with paint scraper
- Applying polyurethane finish with a pad and brush
- Hammering

## TERMS YOU NEED TO KNOW

**REFINISHING FLOORS**—Aggressively sanding floors to entirely remove previous finish and to level the floor before reapplying new floor finish.

**FEATHER SAND**—Sanding with lighter and lighter strokes as you move away from a more heavily sanded area. This creates a smooth transition between sand-ed and non-sanded areas.

**ZIP DOOR**—A plastic sheet with a long vertical zipper. It's taped over entryways for a convenient way to enter and exit rooms for the duration of a project.

## DIFFICULTY LEVEL

SKILLS LEVEL

EASY — MODERATE

This project can be completed in a weekend (not including drying time between finish coats).

# HOW TO REFINISH HARDWOOD FLOORS

**1** Staple plastic on all doorways. Place a zip door over the entryway you plan to use for the duration of the project.

**2** Use painter's tape and plastic to cover heating and cooling registers, ceiling fans, and light fixtures.

**3** Finally, place a fan in a nearby window to blow the circulating dust outside.

## SAFETY FIRST

Even with proper ventilation, inhaling sawdust is a health risk. We recommend getting a respirator. If you don't use one, you must at least wear a dust mask. Eye protection is also a must; and you'll thank yourself for buying a good pair of strong work gloves—they make the sander vibrations a little more bearable.

Important! Always unplug the sander whenever loading or unloading sandpaper.

## SHOPPING TIP: SANDPAPER

| Grits | Grade | Use |
|---|---|---|
| 20, 30, 40, 60 | Course | To level uneven boards. |
| 100, 120 | Medium | To minimize scratches from coarse grits. |
| 150, 180 | Fine | To eliminate scratches from medium grits. |

Sandpaper becomes less effective over time; it may even rip. Buy 3–5 sheets of every grade for each room you want to refinish. You won't use them all, but most rentals allow you to return what you don't use. It's far better to have too many than to find yourself unable to continue until the next day because you ran out and the hardware store is closed.

Reminder: Before you leave the rental shop, have an employee explain to you how to load the paper. Every machine is a little different. See the sidebar on page 124 for some basic instructions.

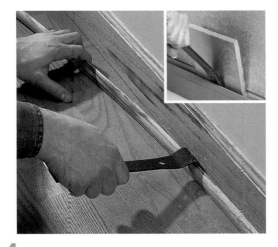

**4** Wedge a pry bar between the shoe molding and baseboards. Move along the wall as nails loosen. Once removed, place a scrap 2 × 4 board against the wall and, with a pry bar, pry out baseboard at nails (inset). Maintain the gap with wood shims. Number the sections for easy replacement. Place wide masking tape along the baseboards. Drive protruding nails in floor ⅛" below the surface with a nail set.

**6** For the initial pass with the drum sander, sand with the grain, using 40- or 60-grit paper; if there are large scratches, use 20 or 30. Start two-thirds down the room length on the right side; work your way to the left. Raise drum. Start motor. Slowly lower drum to floor. Lift the sander off the floor when you reach the wall. Move to the left 2 to 4" and then walk it backwards the same distance you just walked forward. Repeat.

**5** Practice with the drum sander turned off. Move forward and backward. Tilt or raise it off the floor a couple of times. A drum sander is heavy, bulky, and awkward. Once it touches the floor, it walks forward; if you stop it, it gouges the floor.

**7** When you get to the far left side of the room, turn the machine around and repeat the process. Overlap the sanded two-thirds to feather out the ridgeline.

Repeat the sanding process 3 or 4 more times using 120-grit sandpaper. Sand the entire floor. For the final passes, use finer sandpaper (150- to 180-grit) to remove scratches left by coarser papers.

## HERE'S HOW

During the refinishing process it is very likely you will have to change the sandpaper and empty the contents of the dust bag. You should empty the contents of the dust bag when it is two-thirds full. When the machine is turned off, you can see how full the bag is. To check the wear of the sandpaper, turn off your machine every so often and tilt back the machine to check the paper on the underside. If it appears to be thinning, you want to change it.

Correctly replacing the sandpaper can be tricky. A rental professional should be able to walk you through the steps to change the paper and the dust bag, so be sure to consult with him or her before you leave the store.

Power edge sander

**8** To sand hard-to-reach spots, first use a power edge sander along the walls, using the same grit that you last used with the drum sander. Make a succession of overlapping half-circles starting in the corner on one wall. Pull out in an arc and then swirl back to the wall. Continue around the room. Blend together any lines left by the drum and edge sanders by running a rotary buffer over the floor twice: first with an 80-grit screen and then with a 100-grit screen. Finally, use a 5" random orbital sander to smooth out the floor. The random motion naturally feathers out bumps.

**9** Use a paint scraper to get to corners and hard-to-reach nooks and crannies. Pull the scraper toward you with a steady downward pressure. Pull with the grain. Next, sand with a sanding block.

**10** Prepare the room for finish by sweeping and vacuuming. Remove plastic on the doors, windows, and fixtures. Sweep and vacuum again. Wipe up fine particles with a tack cloth.

**11** Apply polyurethane finish. Mix equal parts water-based polyurethane and water. Use a natural bristle brush to apply the mixture along walls and around obstacles. To apply the mixture in the middle of the room, use a painting pad on a pole. Apply 2 coats diagonally across the grain and a final coat in the direction of the grain.

**12** Allow the finish to dry after each coat. Lightly buff the floor with a fine to medium abrasive pad (or buffing pad). Clean the floor with a damp cloth and wipe the area dry with a towel.

**13** Apply at least two coats of undiluted polyurethane finish to get a hard, durable finish. Allow the finish to dry; repeat Step 12 and then add a final coat. Do not overbrush.

**14** After the final coat is dry, buff the surface with water and a fine abrasive pad. This removes surface imperfections and diminishes gloss. After finishing, wait at least 72 hours before replacing the shoe molding. Your newly refinished floor is now complete!

## 24

# Installing Laminate Flooring

The rich wood tones of beautiful laminate planks may cause you to imagine hours of long, hard installation work, but this is a DIY project that you can do in a single weekend. Buy the manufactured planks at a home-improvement or flooring store and install laminate flooring with the step-by-step instructions offered in the following pages.

LAMINATE FLOORING COMES IN A FLOATING SYSTEM THAT IS SIMPLE TO INSTALL, even if you have no experience with other home-improvement projects. You may install a floating laminate floor right on top of plywood, concrete slab, sheet vinyl, or hardwood flooring (follow the manufacturer's instructions). The pieces are available in planks or squares in a variety of different sizes, colors, and faux finishes—including wood and ceramic. Tongue-and-groove edges lock pieces together, and the entire floor floats on the underlayment. At the end of this project there are a few extra steps to take if your flooring manufacturer recommends using glue on the joints.

# LAMINATE JOINTS 101

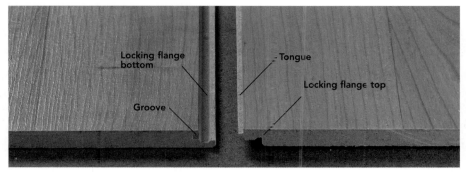

Locking flange bottom — Tongue — Locking flange top — Groove

The joint design for laminate planks and squares is intended to make installation and replacement a breeze, while also providing a barrier from moisture and debris. Today, tongue-and-groove joints are often supplemented with positively locking flanges to provide a tight fit on both the top and bottom of the board. The tongue on one side fits into the groove of the adjacent board; then the the plank is "clicked" into place by pressing down on the plank to join the flanges. Planks without the snap-together ("click") feature sometimes require glue for an extra snug fit (read the manufacturer's instructions carefully and follow all recommendations).

## TERMS YOU NEED TO KNOW

**SUBFLOOR**—The base layer of wood or plywood that supports the underlayment and surface flooring.

**UNDERLAYMENT**—The intermediate layer between the surface floor and the subfloor.

**FLOATING FLOORS**—Floors that are not fastened to the subfloor or underlayment, but rather "float" on top. The flooring is held together with a snap-together, interlocking system.

**GLUELESS LAMINATE FLOORING** (also called "click-floors")—Laminate flooring that does not require glue for installation, but instead relies upon tight tongue-and-groove joints. No-glue flooring is far easier to install and repair than glued laminate flooring, but it may not be as resistant to moisture—so avoid installing it in bathrooms or basements.

**GLUED LAMINATE FLOORING**—Laminate flooring that requires glue at each plank joint in order to effectively seal together the tongue-and-groove planks.

**DRAWBAR**—A metal bar used to pull together the final two planks in a row. There are two hooks—one to attach to the end of a plank close to the wall (where a rubber mallet would not fit to tap the final plank into the adjacent plank), and one on the other end to pull the plank in tight with the adjacent board. See photo in Step 7, page 129.

**STRAP CLAMPS**—A device used to hold several planks together tightly while adhesive in between joints dries. See photo in Step 3, page 133.

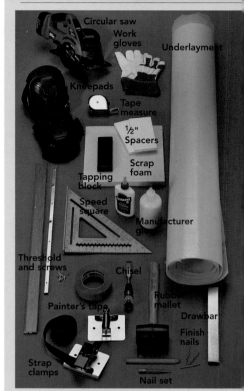
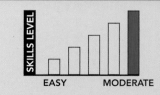

# HOW TO INSTALL LAMINATE FLOORING

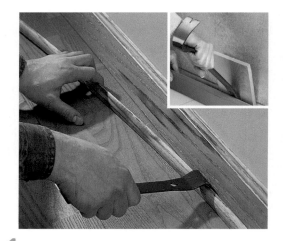

**1** Remove the shoe molding by wedging a pry bar between the shoe molding and baseboards and pry outward. Continue along the wall until the entire shoe is removed. Next, place a scrap board against the wall and use a pry bar to pull the baseboard away from the wall (inset). Maintain the gap with wood shims. Number the sections for easy replacement. Drive protruding nails in floor ⅛" below the surface with a nail set.

**2** To install the underlayment, start in one corner and unroll the underlayment to the opposite wall. Cut the underlayment to fit, using a utility knife or scissors. Overlap the second underlayment sheet according to the manufacturer's recommendations, and secure the pieces in place with adhesive tape.

**3** Working from the left corner of the room to right, set wall spacers and dry lay planks (tongue side facing the wall) against the wall. The spacers allow for expansion. If you are flooring a room more than 26 ft. long or wide, you need to buy appropriate-sized expansion joints. Note: Some manufacturers suggest facing the groove side to the wall.

Final uncut plank
ends here

**4** Set a new plank right side up, on top of the previously laid plank, flush with the spacer against the wall at the end run. Line up a speed square with the bottom plank edge and trace a line. That's the cutline for the final plank in the row.

**5** Press painter's tape along the cutline on the top of the plank to prevent chips when cutting. Score the line drawn in Step 4 with a utility knife. Turn the plank over and extend the pencil line to the backside.

**6** Clamp the board (face down) and rigid foam insulation or plywood to a work table. The foam discourages chipping. Clamp a speed square on top of the plank, as though you are going to draw another line parallel to the cutline—use this to eye your straight cut. Place the circular saw's blade in front (waste side) of the actual cutline.

**7** To create a tight fit for the last plank in the first row, place a spacer against the wall and wedge one end of a drawbar between it and the last plank. Tap the other end of the drawbar with a rubber mallet or hammer. Protect the laminate surface with a thin cloth.

**8** Continue to lay rows of flooring, making sure the joints are staggered. Staggering joints prevents the entire floor from relying on just a few joints, thus preventing the planks from lifting. Staggering also stengthens the floor, because the joints are shorter and evenly distributed.

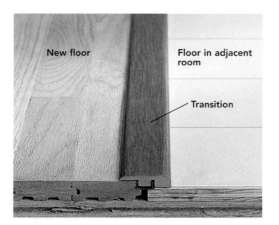

New floor

Floor in adjacent room

Transition

**10** Install transition thresholds at room borders where the new floor joins another floor covering. These thresholds are used to tie together dissimilar floor coverings, such as laminate flooring and wood or carpet. They may also be necessary to span a distance in height between flooring in one room and the next.

**9** To fit the final row, place two planks on top of the last course; slide the top plank up against the wall spacer. Use the top plank to draw a cutline lengthwise on the middle plank. Cut the middle plank to size using the same method as in Step 4 (only now you are "ripcutting" a lengthwise cut—see Here's How on page 133 for instructions on ripcuts). The very last board must be cut lengthwise and widthwise to fit.

### HERE'S HOW

To stagger joints, first check the manufacturer's instructions to determine what the minimum distance should be between the staggered joints. The range is usually between 8" and 18" (minimum). The first plank in the second row can sometimes be the waste piece from the cut you made at the end of the last run. But if you don't have a long enough scrap, the first plank in each row should alternate between being $1/3$ and $2/3$ the length of a full plank. This creates a pattern that is not only pleasing to the eye, but it ensures a solid installation.

# HOW TO WORK AROUND OBSTACLES

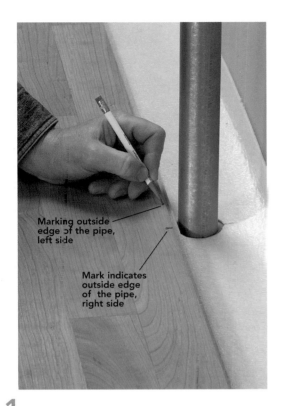

**Marking outside edge of the pipe, left side**

**Mark indicates outside edge of the pipe, right side**

**1** Position a plank end against the spacers on the wall next to the obstacle. Use a pencil to make two marks along the length of the plank, indicating the points where the obstacle begins and ends.

**2** Once the plank is snapped into the previous row, position the plank end against the obstacle. Make two marks with a pencil, this time on the end of the plank to indicate where the obstacle falls along the width of the board.

**3** Use a speed square to extend the four lines. The space at which they all intersect is the part of the plank that needs to be removed to make room for the obstacle to go through it. Use a drill with a Forstner bit, or a hole saw the same diameter as the space within the intersecting lines, and drill through the plank at the X. You'll be left with a hole; extend the cut to the edges with a jigsaw.

**4** Install the plank by locking the tongue-and-groove joints with the preceding board. Fit the end piece in behind the pipe or obstacle. Apply manufacturer-recommended glue to the cut edges, and press the end piece tightly against the adjacent plank. Wipe away excess glue with a damp cloth.

**1** After dry-fitting each row, completely fill the groove of the plank with the manufacturer glue (or at least as instructed by the manufacturer).

**2** Close the gaps between end joints and lengthwise joints, using a rubber mallet to gently tap a block (often supplied by the manufacturer) into the edge or end of the last plank. Use a draw-bar for the last planks butted up to a wall. Wipe away excess glue in the joints with a damp cloth before it dries.

**3** Rent 6 to 10 strap clamps to hold a few rows of planks together as adhesive dries (about an hour). Fit one end of the strap clamp over the plank nearest the wall, and the other end (the one with the ratchet lever) over the last plank. Use the ratchet to tighten straps until joints are snug.

If you need to cut a plank to fit snugly against another plank or a wall with an obstacle in the middle (such as a heat vent), measure in to the appropriate cutline to fit the board flush with the adjacent board or wall (on the other side of the obstacle). Draw a line across the plank in this location. Then measure the obstacle and transfer those measurements to the plank, using your pencil again. Mark a starter hole on the inside of the lines. Drill the hole just large enough to fit your jigsaw blade into it. Starting in the drilled hole, cut the plank along the drawn lines, using a jigsaw. Set the board in place by locking the tongue-and-groove joints with the preceding board.

## WHAT IF . . . ?

**1** Ripcut planks from the back side to avoid splintering the top surface. For accurate straight cuts, mark the cut with a chalk line. If you have drawn a pencil line that is not straight, double check your tracing—it may be that your wall is not perfectly straight, and in this case you'd cut along your hand-drawn pencil line.

**2** Place another piece of flooring next to the piece marked for cutting to provide a stable surface for the foot of the saw. Also, clamp a cutting guide to the planks at the correct distance from the cutting line to ensure a straight cut.

# Installing Self-Adhesive Vinyl Tiles

**25**

Vinyl tiles can be hand-picked to customize your floor. Picking out complementary colors within a single style is one way to make your floor unique. Not only is it fun to design your floor with self-adhesive tiles, but the installation only requires a single weekend.

SELF-ADHESIVE VINYL TILES ARE ESSENTIALLY BIG STICKERS—YOU JUST PEEL off the protective backing and press them into place. Because the tiles are thin, it is important to make sure the subfloor or underlayment is flat and free of debris before installing these tiles. And even though installing these tiles is relatively simple, there are several steps that must be taken to make sure you have a professionally installed floor when all is said and done. We're about to show you just how to do that.

# SELF-ADHESIVE TILES 101

Self-adhesive ("sticky-back") tiles are ready to have the paper backing peeled off and to be immediately stuck to the floor. They do not require adhesive.

## TERMS YOU NEED TO KNOW

SUBFLOOR—The base layer of wood or plywood that supports the underlayment and surface flooring.

UNDERLAYMENT—The intermediate layer between the surface flooring material and the subfloor.

REFERENCE LINES—Reference lines mark the center of the room and divide it into quadrants.

LAYOUT LINES—Layout lines are based on reference lines but are adjusted to produce the fewest number of narrow tiles around the perimeter of the room (i.e., making the layout symmetrical).

STICKY-BACK VINYL TILE—Resilient flooring available in 12" or 16" squares. Each vinyl tile has self-adhesive backing.

EMBOSSING LEVELER—Used to prepare resilient flooring, provided it is well adhered to the subfloor, for use as new floor covering underlayment.

## TOOLS & SUPPLIES YOU NEED

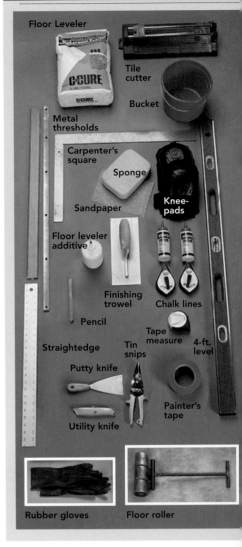

Floor Leveler
Tile cutter
Bucket
Metal thresholds
Carpenter's square
Sponge
Sandpaper
Knee-pads
Floor leveler additive
Finishing trowel
Chalk lines
Pencil
Tape measure
4-ft. level
Straightedge
Tin snips
Putty knife
Utility knife
Painter's tape

Rubber gloves        Floor roller

## SKILLS YOU NEED

- Measuring
- Cutting
- Pushing a 75- or 100-pound floor roller
- Using a trowel
- Hammering

## DIFFICULTY LEVEL

EASY        MODERATE

This project can be completed in a weekend.

**1** Check to make sure your floor is level with a 4-ft. level. If there are dips or low spots in plywood subfloors, mix leveler according to the manufacturer's directions. Make sure your floor is free of debris before proceeding by sweeping and/or vacuuming.

**3** Use a 4-ft. level to make sure the patch is level with the surrounding area. Add more level, if necessary. Allow the level to dry, then shave off any ridges with the edge of the trowel, or sand the area smooth.

**2** Use a finishing trowel to spread a thin coat of leveler over the surface of the floor. Hold the trowel close to the surface of the floor to make a thin, consistent coating. Cover all depressions. The leveler will start to set within 10 minutes, so work quickly.

### WHAT IF . . . ?

Floor leveler is used to fill in subtle imperfections—such as dips and low spots—in plywood subfloors. If your subfloor is made of dimensional lumber, rather than plywood, you must use plywood to patch damaged sections—contact a floor specialist to look at your floor if this is the case.

**4** First measure each wall, marking the width and length center points. Align one end of a chalk line with the center point on one wall and align the other end with the center point on the opposing wall. It's easiest to have two people holding each end, so you can grab the line between two fingers, lift it up a few inches, and let it snap to the floor. We'll call this line X.

Line Y

Line X

**5** To create a second chalk line, measure the length of chalk line X and mark its center point. Place the corner of a carpenter's square at this point. Align the chalk line with the square and snap a line. We'll call this line Y. The framing square ensures line Y is perpendicular to line X.

5 ft.

4 ft.

3 ft.

90°

**6** Test your lines to make sure they're perpendicular. Make a mark 3 ft. from the center point of line X. Make a mark 4 ft. from the center point of line Y. Measure the distance between the marks. If X and Y are perpendicular, the distance between them is 5 ft. If not, adjust them until they're perpendicular.

## WHAT IF . . . ?

If you want to create a diagonal layout rather than the standard layout, you'll need to snap a diagonal line. Make a mark 5 ft. from the center point of each reference line. Snap chalk lines to connect these points. Snapping a longer chalk line over it divides the room into perfect quadrants. A diagonal layout requires more tile cutting along the edges; but if that's what you want, it's not so difficult that you should choose the square layout just because it's easier.

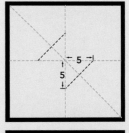

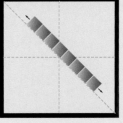

**7** If border tiles are equal, then the reference lines are the layout lines, and you can continue to dry-fit the entire quadrant. (If the last tiles are less than half a tile width from the wall, you need to adjust the chalk lines to make the borders equal—see Step 9.)

**8** Start at the intersection of X and Y and dry-fit tiles along each line out to all four walls.

---

**HERE'S HOW**

Allow your vinyl tiles to acclimate to the room's temperature before you install them. Since vinyl tile can shrink or expand with changes in temperature or humidity, it's best to have the tiles sit in the room they will be installed in for a day or so before starting the project.

**9** To adjust the chalk lines, create a new line (we'll call it X1) by lining up the tiles along line Y so the gaps are equal at both ends. The joint between the two tiles nearest line X is your new line. This is your layout line. Use a different color chalk to avoid confusion.

**10** To install the tiles, peel off the paper backing and install the tile in one of the corners formed by the intersecting layout lines. Rub the entire surface of the tile to bond the adhesive to the floor. Lay the tiles along each layout line in the quadrant. Work from the center of the room toward the walls. Make sure the tiles fit together tightly—there should be no gaps between the joints.

### WHAT IF . . . ?

If the tile sticks before you wanted to place it, slide a wide-blade putty knife underneath to pry it up. Discard the tile and use a new one. Unlike tiles laid in adhesive, which can be wiggled to fit into position, sticky-back tiles cannot be moved once they are placed.

**11** Finish setting all of the full tiles in the first quadrant before creating reference lines for the next quadrant. Do this for all four quadrants. The partial tiles at corners and borders are dealt with last.

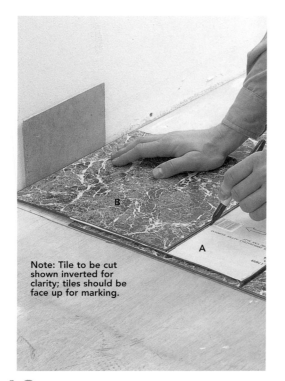

Note: Tile to be cut shown inverted for clarity; tiles should be face up for marking.

**12** To cut tiles to fit along the walls, place the tile to be cut (A) face up on top of the last full tile you installed. Position a spacer against the wall, then set a marker tile (B) on top of the tile to be cut. Trace along the edge of the marker tile to draw a cutting line.

**13** To mark tiles for cutting around outside corners, make a cardboard template to match the space, keeping a gap (the size of your spacer) along the walls. After cutting the template, check to make sure it fits. Place the template on a tile and trace its outline.

### TOOL TIP

If the vinyl tile is too thick for the utility knife to cut through it, use a ceramic-tile cutter. Mark the cutting line on the backside of the tile with a marker, then place the tile in the cutter so the cutting wheel is directly over the line. While pressing down on the wheel handle, run the wheel across the tile to cut it. Press with even pressure across the entire tile, so you only have to move the cutting wheel across the tile once.

**14** Use a utility knife and straightedge to cut along the marked line on the corner (or border) tile. It's important to individually measure and cut each tile. If you precut a bunch of tiles before installing them, you are going to run into difficulties. Most walls are not perfectly straight, so the amount you have to cut from each tile may change as you move along the wall.

**15** Dry-fit the tiles to make sure your cuts are straight and the tile fits in place snugly. Remove the paper backing and lay the tiles in place.

**16** Once the flooring is completely installed, use a flooring roller to set the tiles. Roll over the entire floor in a vertical and then horizontal direction, to completely set each tile in place. A flooring roller can be rented from your local home-improvement store.

**17** Measure the threshold width. Cut the threshold to size, using tin snips. Position each bar over the edge of the vinyl flooring and nail it in place.

# INDEX

## Photo Credits

© Royalty-Free/Corbis: cover, pp. 24, 80

Photo Courtesy of Kemiko Concrete Stains: p. 112
Kemiko Concrete Stains
www.Kemiko.com
903-587-3708
Leonard, TX

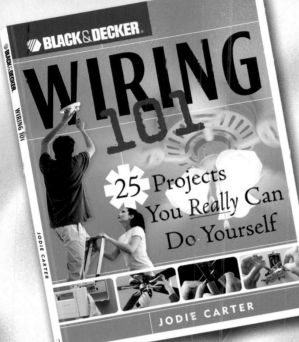
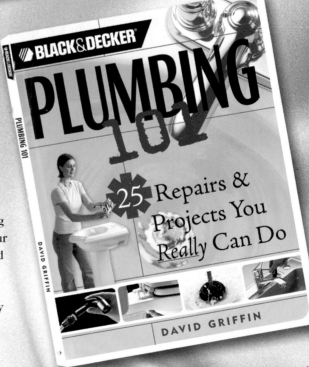

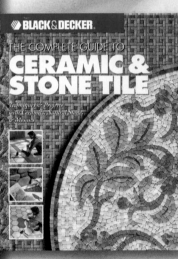